Swindon Decoded

Swindon Decoded

The Curious History of a Remarkable Town

John Chandler

First published in the United Kingdom in 1992 as *Swindon: history and guide*, by Alan Sutton Publishing; 2nd edition, published by The Hobnob Press in 2005. This revised, expanded and partly rewritten 3rd edition published in 2023

by The Hobnob Press,
8 Lock Warehouse, Severn Road, Gloucester GL1 2GA
www.hobnobpress.co.uk

© John Chandler, text and images, 2023

The Author hereby asserts his moral rights to be identified as the Author of the Work.

All rights reserved. No part of this publication may be reproduced, stored in a retrieval system, or transmitted in any form or by any means, electronic, mechanical, photocopying, recording or otherwise, without the prior permission of the publisher and copyright holder.

British Library Cataloguing in Publication Data
A catalogue record for this book is available from the British Library

ISBN 978-1-914407-60-4

Typeset in Chaparral Pro, 11/14 pt
Typesetting and origination by John Chandler

Except where stated, all modern photographs were taken by the author between 2020 and 2023.

Front cover artwork: Murray John Tower, by Simon Dennis ~ www.artbysi.co.uk.

Title page: View from Dixon Street, by Samuel Loxton, c.1910 (Swindon Libraries).

CONTENTS

	Introduction	1
1	Swindon Landscapes	10
2	But a Small Place	33
3	The First Push	51
4	A God of Steam	71
5	Brick-Built Breeding Boxes	95
6	Evening Star and Sunrise	115
7	No Mean City?	131
	Strolling around Swindon	147
8	The Hilltop Town	149
9	The Railway Estate	163
10	Growing Pains	173
11	Travels through Suburbia	187
	Delving Deeper	195
	Acknowledgements	199
	Index	200

About the Author

JOHN CHANDLER was born in 1951 and brought up in Devon. He studied classics at the University of Bristol, and was awarded his doctorate for research there on ancient history in 1977. Between 1974 and 1988 he worked for Wiltshire County Council, in Swindon and Amesbury, and from 1979 as Local Studies Librarian, based at Trowbridge. Since 1988 he has worked as a freelance historical researcher, writer, editor and lecturer, latterly (since 2011) for the Victoria County History in Gloucestershire and Wiltshire. He has written or edited more than twenty books, including histories of Salisbury, Swindon, the Vale of Pewsey, Shaftesbury Abbey and churches in Wiltshire, and editions of the travellers John Leland and John Taylor. He is a Fellow of the Society of Antiquaries, a Visiting Research Fellow of the University of the West of England, and a publisher of books on local and regional history. He lives in Gloucester. *Website:* www.hobnobpress.co.uk.

INTRODUCTION

DOWN THERE ALONGSIDE Basingstoke and Bognor, Scunthorpe and Wigan, Swindon is a place to be made fun of – clone town, crap town, handy town whenever a London journalist, short on originality, needs somewhere to be rude about.

But why? Is it the name? Well admittedly Swindon probably does mean 'pig hill'.* And yes, viewed from the rest of Wiltshire Swindon does have a kind of alien quality – a form of civilization, but not as others know it.

I first became acquainted with Swindon almost fifty years ago, when I worked for a year in the central reference library in Regent Circus. I have fondish memories of the place, particularly of the evening shift (we were open until 9 in those days). There were the old men after 'yesterday's Adver'' (they weren't allowed to read the current issue, so always had their local news a day late),** rock concert rehearsals going on in the room upstairs while we were trying to keep the peace below, innocent flirting with the library assistants, and attempting (just as inexpertly, and once with painful consequences) to eject drunks.

And yet that year also nurtured in me an affection and respect for the place, born out of curiosity, I suppose. The civic pride was palpable; there was that no-nonsense dignity of a workaday town that could produce solid, heavy, complicated machines; and there were mysterious new industries arriving – polymers and electronics – bowled along by the recently completed motorway.

---

* John Aubrey's Latin derivation, *Mons Porcorum*, though spurious no doubt, should perhaps be revived, to give the town a certain *gravitas*.
**The *Evening Advertiser*, now *Swindon Advertiser*, a daily evening paper.

But there was also something wrong. I remember strolling out on my first lunch-break and looking for the town centre. There didn't seem to be one. Towns I was used to had a square with a church nearby and busy streets leading in from all directions. Nothing like that here. Of course a few days later I discovered such a place, up on the hill, but it was nowhere near what I perceived to be the centre – decidedly eccentric, in fact.

Perhaps it was that observation that started me on a lifetime's interest in urban topography – the shape, history and growth of towns. How, merely by looking around and some historical detective work, can we make sense of the places where we live? Years later, with several town histories to my name and others in progress, I was approached by a publisher to write a short history of, and guide to, a Wiltshire town. Swindon seemed my obvious choice. It was published in 1992, sold modestly, was well reviewed, languished for a while, and then went out of print.

A shame, I thought, and as authors always do, I blamed the publisher. By the time of my second attempt I was a publisher myself. I revised and retitled my book, and produced a slim, pocket edition in 2005. Now, still publishing, and with greatly improved printing technology, it is time for a third edition, enlarged and in colour.

Swindon's history is extraordinary, weird, unique; but it is like a code, needing a key to decipher it. So my book is in two parts. The first seven chapters present the history of Swindon in roughly the order that things happened, from geological beginnings to more-or-less the present, and scattering on the way the clues which, in four more chapters, I use to try to decipher the past. So we (writer and reader) make the switch from being historians, surrounded by books and documents, to becoming topographers – or *flaneurs* (in the more casual French way) – observers of the streets and buildings and their occupants, as we walk around decoding our town.

Swindon is a work in progress. All towns are, if there is any life in them. And Swindon certainly has life. My take on how to understand Swindon, affectionate but somewhat detached (I've never lived here – though I'm tempted to) relies heavily on the labours of others, historians who have spent many years unravelling their native or adopted town, and whose names appear in my acknowledgements.

INTRODUCTION

So this is to some extent an outsider's view, but first writing this book all those years ago made me a Swindon enthusiast. And maybe reading about it will make you one too. Because, after all, Swindon like any town needs people to understand and become enthusiastic about it. So I LIKE Swindon – and I am not alone. If you don't, maybe you just have not understood why it is the way it is. Read my book and perhaps you will find out.

John Chandler
October 2023

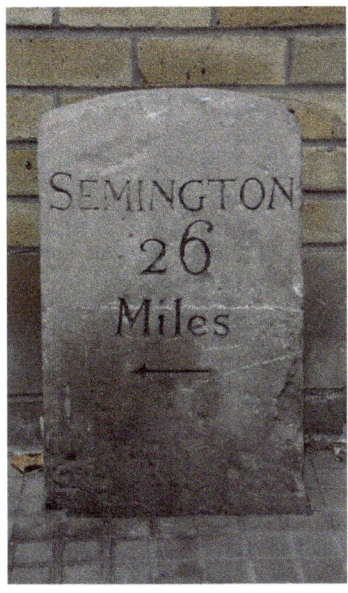

1
SWINDON LANDSCAPES

SWINDON IS BEST approached from the south. Driving up from Devizes, after many miles of downland the traveller begins to descend, and a different world is suddenly revealed. Beyond the flat green patchwork of Wroughton's rectangular fields and an incessant motorway there are houses and factories, office blocks and warehouses, building sites and a church spire. Go up there and sit in that lay-by where the view begins and you can watch Swindon wake up. It is 7 o'clock on a spring morning, and the sun is dissolving a light lingering mist in preparation for another hot day. With binoculars you can make out the

hazy outline of higher ground, the Corallian ridge on which Purton, Blunsdon and Stratton are perched, and you can see that in places the houses extend up to and over this temporary horizon. Later the mist will clear, to reveal Braydon Forest and the Cotswolds beyond. In front of you a broad low hill rises from the valley to mask the longer view; it was this limestone eminence which gave Swindon its name, and it was here that Old Swindon, or High Swindon, was built. To its right you can make out more offices and factories, and you know that behind them is rolled a carpet of houses far further than the eye can see.

Of the many hundreds of buildings discernible through the mist perhaps only a dozen are more than two centuries old, and they are almost all outside Swindon – at Wroughton and Elcombe in the foreground. Away to the left Toothill, Freshbrook and the other West Swindon neighbourhoods have all arrived since I occasionally used to cycle along there to work from Wootton Bassett forty-something years ago. Wichelstowe, just beyond the motorway, is a new village, entirely of the 21st century. Swindon itself had a population below 2,000 until about 1840; now, including Stratton, it has surpassed 200,000, a hundredfold increase. – Remarkable! Perhaps, therefore, this book should begin in 1840.

But that would be quite wrong. The landscape itself, on which modern Swindon so recently sits, has been shaped and modified

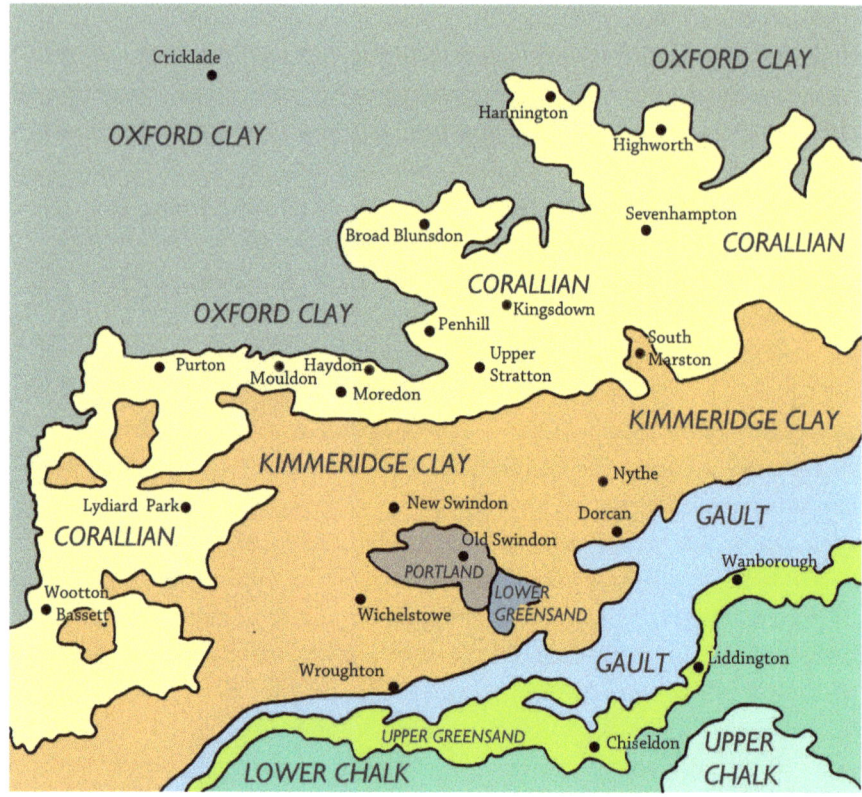

by men and women since prehistory, and here and there (and more than most people imagine) traces of their handiwork show through. So anyone wishing to decode modern Swindon must begin with the landscapes beneath, from their geological origins through centuries of agriculture and rural settlement, up to the point at which they became 'Swindonised'. That is what this chapter aims to do. In chapters two and three we shall look at the successive communities which have lived at the heart of these landscapes, on Swindon Hill itself; and from chapter four onwards we shall enter the world of railways, suburbs and urban life generally, the Swindon which we know today.

Southern England's terrain results from a sequence of rocks formed as sediment on the ocean floor. The chemical composition of each stratum depends on various factors, including the nature of the riverborne material being carried into the ocean at the time, and the organisms which the water could sustain. Geological forces have buckled the strata, and climatic forces have eroded them, so that different rocks break the land surface in different places, and have succumbed in various ways to the effects of water, frost and vegetation. A line drawn on a map across the Swindon area, from Chiseldon in the south-east to Cricklade in the north-west, represents a journey back through geological time, as different rocks are encountered, each older than the one before. The downland above Chiseldon and Wroughton, around the lay-by where I have absent-mindedly left you sitting, is made of chalk, the youngest rock in the sequence. Below this chalk the line traverses greensands and clays, then the Corallian limestone, then older clays beyond. Because of their different properties the rocks manifest themselves in different ways – the chalk as well-drained rounded hills, the heavy clays as flat valleys, often waterlogged, the limestone as an irregular ridge, and so on.

This may be an over-simplification, but it explains much of the landscape structure seen from the lay-by above Wroughton. It does not account for Swindon Hill, however, which at its western limit stands up proud from the clay, and which extends eastwards almost to the chalk beyond Broome. This hill is largely composed of Portland and Purbeck Beds, fine building limestones which occur also in south Wiltshire and Dorset. Their presence here is explained by a syncline, or concave fold, in the clay at this point, which beneath the ocean filled up with deep deposits of shelly sediment. The deposits compacted to form these hard limestones, which are more resistant to weathering than the surrounding clays, and so have been left standing high and dry above the valley.

The underlying geology has determined not only the scenery, but also the vegetation which grows on its soil. The lighter soils of the chalk hillsides and the limestone ridges are better for arable cultivation than the sticky clay, and these must have been heavily exploited for growing crops during later prehistory. In general subsequent centuries of farming have obliterated the archaeological evidence, but at the margins left untouched by the medieval plough, such as on Burderop Down below the hillfort at Barbury, a network of small field boundaries survives as earthworks to show just how far up the hillside the prehistoric arable farmer was prepared to go. The claylands provided other resources – woodland for building, fuel and pannage, clay for pottery, and, when cleared, grassland for pasturing cattle.

Geology helps to explain Swindon – so too does archaeology. Building above ground involves disturbance below, and the pace of the town's expansion and renewal, especially since the 1970s, has required digging thousands of holes in the ground. Under watchful archaeological eyes, and in many cases preceded by controlled excavation, Swindon's soil has been coaxed into yielding a rich haul of artefacts, samples and structures spanning millennia – far more than if it had been left alone. From this harvest it is possible to discover who has lived here and what they did to their surroundings.

Stray flints worked more than 12,000 years ago have been found now and then, but tangible evidence for settlements only becomes widespread as the population increased towards the end of the Bronze Age, around 1,000 BC, and then on into the succeeding Iron Age. A glimpse of farming life in the Swindon landscape during the Iron Age was provided by archaeological discoveries made in 1976-7, when the Groundwell Farm industrial estate was being built. A sequence of four round wooden houses within an enclosure was excavated, together with

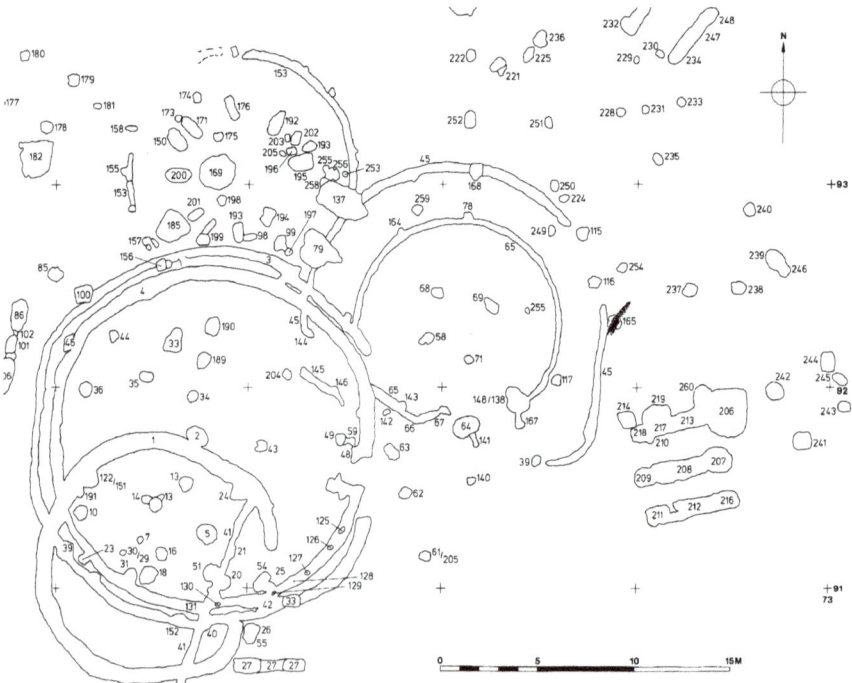

A plan of excavated Iron Age features at Groundwell Farm, including a sequence of four round houses. (WANHS) A reconstruction model of the largest (opposite) was made for display in Swindon Museum. (Swindon Museum / Bernard Phillips).

granaries and other farm buildings. From pottery and animal bone it seemed that this was the working farm of a single family, and was in use from after 500 BC until before 200 BC. Their farming economy was mixed, and combined crop-growing (probably using oxen as draught animals) with the rearing of sheep and pigs. Pig bones were more numerous than on similar sites elsewhere, and this suggests that they were using woodland on the adjacent clays for pannage. The farmers seem to have been quite poor, since few metal implements were in use, and after the house and farmyard had been abandoned for several centuries the site was cleared and put down to arable, probably before AD 100. Swindon Museum has a reconstruction model of Groundwell Iron-Age farm.

Groundwell was probably typical of many small farms dotted around the Swindon landscape in later prehistory, and several more have been investigated since, at Moredon, Shaw, South Marston, and a second site at Groundwell. They came and went, and some, such as a larger settlement excavated at Cleveland Farm, Ashton Keynes, continued as native communities during the centuries of Roman occupation. The

Saxon place-name Walcot, which means something like 'the huts of the natives', may refer to one such settlement, and so this settlement must have survived beyond the end of the Roman period and still have been in use several centuries later (*Wal-* is related to our names Wales and Welsh, and was used by English-speaking Saxons to describe the native ethnic Celts whom they lived alongside or supplanted). By their activities, clearing woodland, manuring soil, making and consolidating tracks, building houses and marking out territories, the prehistoric and Roman farmers doubtless modified the landscape in ways which still affect modern Swindon; but how many of our modern roads and administrative boundaries owe their idiosyncrasies to such distant ancestors we shall probably never know.

Apart from the downland hillforts and field systems the oldest tangible pieces of human endeavour in the Swindon area are two Roman

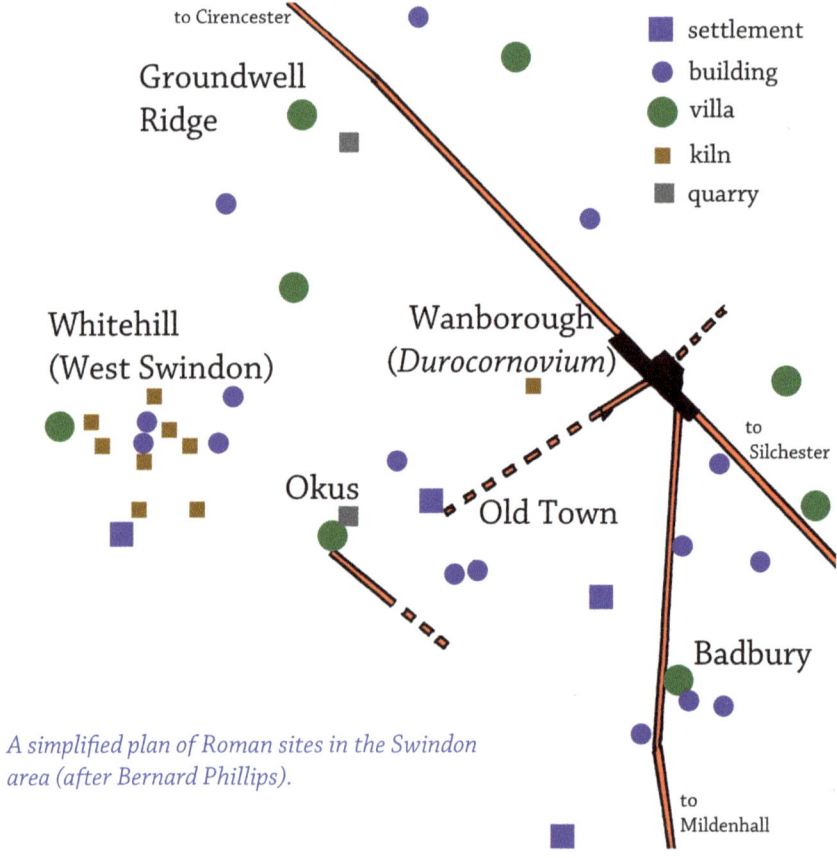

A simplified plan of Roman sites in the Swindon area (after Bernard Phillips).

The name of the Roman town, Durocornovium, was preserved as Dorcan through the Saxon and medieval centuries because of the Dorcan brook, which flows here. As Swindon expanded eastwards in the late 20th century the ancient name was adopted for a largely industrial suburb.

roads. Ermin Street, as part of the route from London to Cirencester is known, and another road (referred to in the Saxon period as Broken Street) which ran north from the Roman town at Mildenhall, near Marlborough, to meet it near Covingham, have both been superimposed over parts of their route by the A419 dual carriageway. In fact part of the latter was uncovered in 2005, preserved in the centre of the Commonhead roundabout when it was 'improved' into a flyover. The topography of Stratton St Margaret is patently dominated by the line of Ermin Street, and this link with Rome is a matter of local pride and folk etymology. 'You know what Stratton means, don't you?' I was once told by an elderly inhabitant, '– straight on!'. The name, which is Saxon, does indeed refer to Ermin Street, but not quite so blatantly: it means 'farm by the paved road'.

Few motorists today, belting round Swindon up the A419 from the Commonhead flyover, probably have time to ponder the fact that the bend in the road's direction from north to north-west is actually caused by the junction of Roman roads, nor that the name of the area to their left, Dorcan, is in fact a distant echo of the small town, *Durocornovium*, which Roman administrators established at that road junction. Part of this settlement was explored between 1966 and 1976, before much of it disappeared under the dual carriageway. The excavations suggested that a small community arrived here soon after the Roman road was built, clustered around a military installation. Later, in the second century a *mansio* was built north of the road junction. This was an official staging-post for Roman soldiers, messengers and other government staff – a kind of exclusive Macdonalds-cum-Travelodge for pass-holders only. Along the main road and in a grid of streets around the *mansio* a considerable town grew up, with market hall, stalls and workshops. Undaunted by the low-lying terrain on the floodplain (their timber-framed houses were built on solid stone foundations) a community of craftsmen flourished in the third and fourth centuries AD, providing goods and services for the main road travellers, and a market for the surrounding countryside, including the whole of what has become the Swindon area. Their town extended along Ermin Street for about a mile and was home perhaps to 1,000-1,500 inhabitants.

The countryside around this 'proto-Swindon', *Durocornovium*, included not only the homesteads of small farmers, partially Romanised but still in the native Iron-Age mould, but also two other groups who arrived in the wake of Roman prosperity. From a little before 100 AD potters colonised the claylands and began to produce cooking pots, jars and other coarse pottery for the *Durocornovium* market and further afield. To date nine kiln sites and twenty-four separate kilns have been discovered, as West Swindon housing and industrial development has

An artist's recostruction of activity at the West Swindon Roman kilns site (Alison Borthwick).

spread since the 1970s across the countryside towards Purton (one area has been named Kiln Park to commemorate their work). Here not only the local clay could be exploited, but there was also ample woodland for fuel to fire the kilns, so that not only kilns, but also houses and an infrastructure of paved roads could be laid out. The industry, which probably supplied tiles for building as well as domestic pottery, had affinities with other production centres, at Gloucester and in Savernake Forest, and continued in operation until the end of the Roman period after 400 AD.

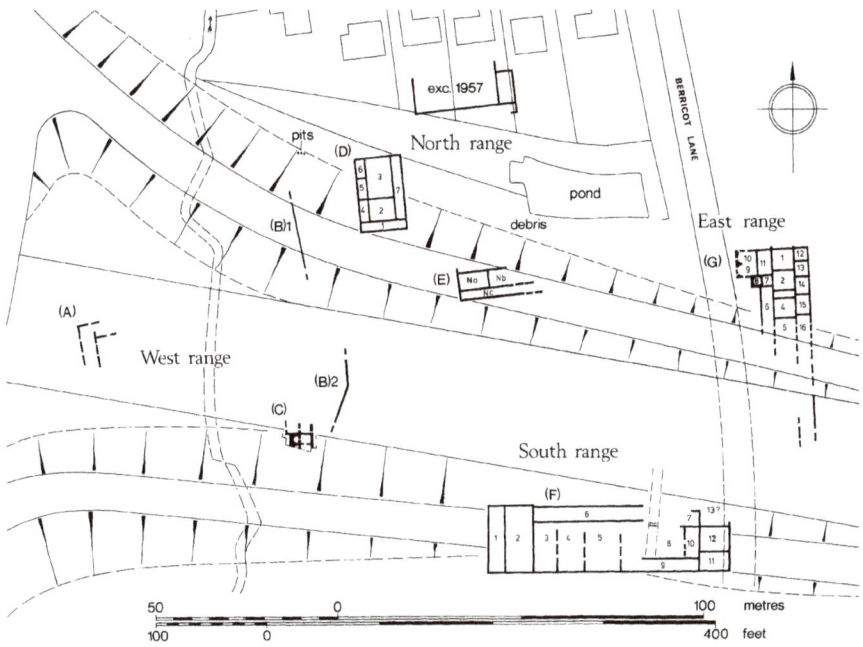

Plan of the Badbury Roman villa excavation, hastily undertaken as the eastern slip roads for M4 junction 15 (also plotted) were under construction (WANHS).

The other group to emerge around *Durocornovium*, as elsewhere, was a class of sophisticated farmer–landowners, who reorganised local agriculture on the basis of the villa estate. Evidence of Roman villas, either the structures themselves or the trappings of luxury which accompanied them, have been found in various places around Swindon, including Purton, Stanton Fitzwarren, Wanborough, Chiseldon and elsewhere. One of the largest known villa complexes in the area, and among the largest in England, lay next to the Roman road at Badbury.

It was partially and very inadequately excavated during motorway construction between 1969 and 1971, and was found to have flourished almost throughout the Roman period. It included luxurious living apartments and working buildings spaced across an area of some two hectares, which is now largely beneath motorway junction 15 and its access roads.

But even this was overshadowed by the discovery in 1996 of a complex of Roman buildings on Groundwell Ridge, during preliminary work for the Abbey Meads sector of Swindon's northern expansion. The site, on sloping ground facing south, is close to Blunsdon St Andrew, and less than a kilometre from Ermin Street. Excavations over parts of the area from its discovery until 2005 revealed extensive and opulent underfloor-heated suites of rooms and bath-houses, suggesting a Roman villa on the largest and richest scale; but the complex also included some kind of shrine, apparently dedicated to the exotic eastern goddess Isis, built around the natural springs issuing from the hillside. Whether

Groundwell Ridge, site of a major Roman villa discovered in 1996 and subsequently excavated. The area was rescued from housing development and kept as an open space, with fine views southwards over Swindon to the Marlborough Downs.

religious or residential, or both, the site was recognised as of such national as well as local significance that in 1999 it was bought back from the developer by Swindon Borough Council, so as to preserve the archaeology and create a public amenity – a far cry from the treatment meted out to Badbury villa thirty years earlier.

The owners of Groundwell, Badbury and the other villa-estates must have formed a powerful local aristocracy, and when the edifice of Roman rule, including their small town, crumbled in the fifth century, they did not immediately disappear. At Badbury, for instance, life under reduced circumstances appears to have continued in the east range of buildings for a considerable time; and at Groundwell later timber-framing has been found on top of Roman brickwork. Some of the landholdings associated with Roman villas may have remained as viable economic units through all the turmoil, only to reappear several hundred years later under Saxon landlords.

Up to this point almost everything we can decode about human activity in the Swindon countryside derives from archaeology. Only one clue has come from a document, but it is a significant one, the name of the Roman town *Durocornovium* – important because it explains why a modern suburb has come to be called Dorcan. But from now on documents will start to become available, and soon they will be our main sources of information.

We learn of the boundaries of the fledgling Saxon estates from surviving copies of the documents which conveyed them from one owner to another. Moredon, for example, now a Swindon suburb, first makes its appearance on the stage of written history in 758, when the king of Wessex granted land there to Malmesbury Abbey. Nearly two centuries later, in 943, Moredon occurs in another charter, this time with a description of its boundaries.

Most of these boundaries can still be traced on the ground. They begin at a place called *Higford*, 'the hay ford', which was probably close to where Northern Road now crosses the Rodbourne Stream. This stream, called *Hreod Burna*, 'the reedy brook', still lives up to its Saxon name in places, and the boundary ran west along it as far as its confluence with the River Ray (near the Purton Road/ Thamesdown Drive interesction). Next we can follow it north down the river to Tadpole Lane (by the station on the Swindon to Cricklade railway), then running east around

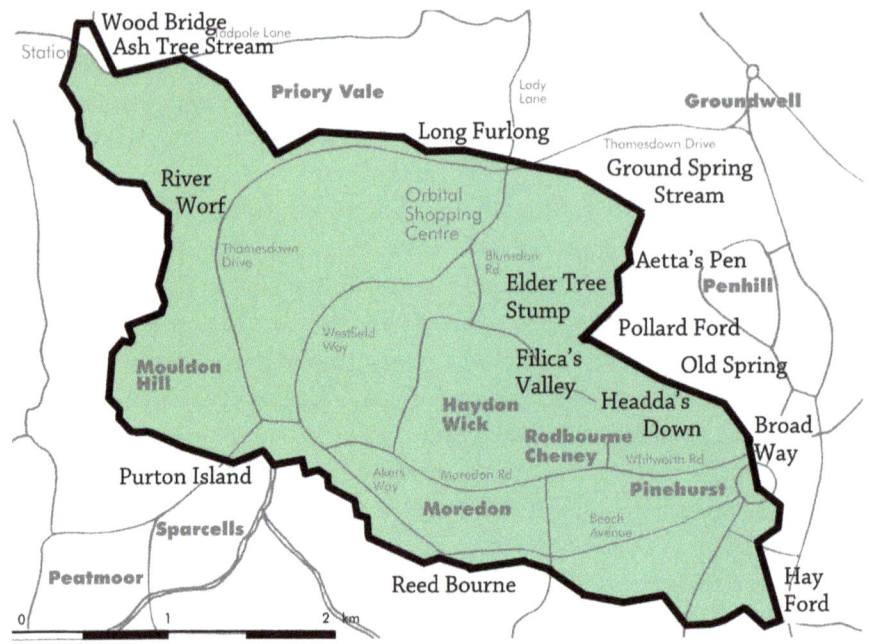

The Saxon boundaries of an estate called Moredon, which now pick their way through modern housing estates.

the new Priory Vale development at North Swindon to Lady Lane; from there it was marked by what the charter calls 'an old ditch' as far as the foot of Penhill. After this it turned south, and tracing it among the houses of Haydon Wick and Pinehurst becomes more difficult. At some point it crossed the *Bradan Weg*, or 'wide way', which is presumably the modern Whitworth Road, and the name has been kept in use by the adjacent road, Broadway.

Moredon's charter, surveyed and written down over a millennium ago, defines an area uncannily similar to that of Swindon's northern expansion, begun during the late twentieth century and now complete. And it is only one of several relating to places around Swindon which have survived. Others describe Purton, Badbury, Wanborough and part of Wroughton. Doubtless many more once existed which now are lost, setting out in meticulous detail the twists and turns of Swindon's ancient boundaries.

To the historian the survivors are important for two reasons.

In the first place they offer a kind of bridge between the territories of prehistory and the villa-owners on the one hand, and the later parishes and administrative units on the other, which have in turn shaped the development of towns like Swindon. In the second place they are repositories of Saxon place-names – often the direct ancestors of the modern names in daily use – which are themselves little capsules of information about Saxon landscape, people and settlements.

Familiar names which first occur in documents more than a thousand years ago include Groundwell ('the deep spring') and Chiseldon ('the gravel valley'). Three others – Moredon, Mannington and Ellendun – include the Saxon name element *dun*, which means 'hill', specifically places on high ground already occupied as settlements before the Saxons arrived. Likewise Lydiard and Penhill probably embody much older, Celtic, words for 'ridge' and 'promontory' respectively in use by the native population. At least ten other place-names around Swindon, including Swindon itself, are first recorded in Domesday Book in 1086, although they are likely by then to have been in use already for many years. Other names, not found until documents proliferate in the thirteenth century, were probably also first coined several centuries before. Most seem to be telling us about their position relative to the geological differences of limestone, chalk and clay which we explored earlier. Thus a row of *dun* names is sprinkled along the Corallian ridge – Mouldon, Moredon, Haydon, Blunsdon, Kingsdown – whereas several clayland names suggest waterlogged or wooded conditions; they include Nythe ('land surrounded by water') and South Marston ('farm in the marsh') east of Swindon, and Shaw ('wood'), Sparcells ('wood for spears or spars') and Blagrove ('black thicket') to the west. Mannington (possibly 'Mehha's hill'), Chaddington ('Ceatta's hill') and Toothill ('the look-out hill') all seem to refer to minor eminences rising from the clay. The derivation of Swindon, 'the hill where pigs are kept', is well known, and refers of course to the limestone ridge on which Old Town sits.

You may have noticed, when we explored the Saxon estate of Moredon, 'the hill of waste land', that the name of one prominent feature had already been used to denote the whole territory, almost all of North Swindon in fact, even though much of it lay alongside sluggish rivers and among sticky wood pasture, for which 'Moredon' was a quite inappropriate description. When in Domesday Book we find

The parish church of Blunsdon, one of the many places perched along the Corallian ridge which embody their hilltop position in their names.

the name Swindon for the first time it had likewise come to be used for a considerable area, embracing in fact much of the large medieval parish, and consisting of five or six distinct landholdings. Thus separate names came into use for some of its constituent parts, such as Eastcott, Westcott and Nethercott ('the eastern, western and lower groups of cottages'), as well as the tautological Even Swindon. This literally means 'the hill of pigs on the flat ground', which would be nonsense, but of course what it really denotes is 'the flat portion of the Swindon estate'. By the thirteenth century, when Even Swindon is first recorded, we also find the expression 'High Swindon' in use to describe the area on the hill.

Around the time of Domesday Book, or a little before, the old Saxon estates became bound up with new territorial creations, the ecclesiastical parishes. The modern Swindon conurbation embraces most of three ancient parishes – Swindon itself, Rodbourne Cheney (which included Moredon and Haydon), and Stratton St Margaret – and has in recent years nibbled away at the clayland holdings of several others, such as Liddington, Wroughton, Blunsdon, South Marston and the Lydiards.

SWINDON LANDSCAPES

A parish might include several landholdings or manors – often the successors of Saxon estates – and the subsequent history and ownership of Swindon's Domesday manors have been meticulously traced. Their evolution need not concern us too much here, although we shall see further on how, even as late as the 1870s, manorial divisions had a crucial effect on determining where and when Swindon could expand. But two other topics on which manorial history impinges, medieval settlements and agriculture, do demand our attention at this point.

Evidence from archaeology, manorial records and medieval tax lists enables us to build up a picture of where people were living around Swindon and how they were supporting themselves. The larger and more

The three ancient parishes, and their neighbours, over which modern Swindon extends.

Swindon's manors at Domesday in 1086 included Nethercott, which after the Norman conquest had been given to one of the king's close associates, Bishop Odo of Bayeux. His tenant was a man called Wadard. Remarkably, we have portraits of both men, as they are depicted on the Bayeux Tapestry.

prosperous communities were those to be found on the chalk slopes or the limestone ridge. Here, at places such as Chiseldon, Wanborough, Stratton and Blunsdon, villages were established which have continued to the present day. Several of these hillside villages, in addition to their fields of good arable land on chalky or sandy soil, possessed areas of clay vale which they attempted to exploit as pasture grounds. The name-element *wic* is thought by most experts to denote a secondary settlement or farmstead concentrated on dairying, and so we find Liddington Wick (now beneath the Eldene estate), Haydon Wick (also now submerged beneath houses), Badbury Wick, and Wick Farm at West Swindon (formerly belonging to Lydiard Millicent) all down on the clay below their parent communities. Swindon's own satellite hamlets on the claylands were probably little more than single farmsteads. In 1377 only 45 adult taxpayers lived in the combined territory of Eastcott, Westcott and Walcot, and another 27 in Even Swindon. These figures compare with 248 on Swindon Hill and 160 at Stratton St Margaret.

The fourteenth century was in general a time of retrenchment and shrinking population after many generations of growth. Among the poorer communities in the Swindon area some, such as Rodbourne Cheney and Even Swindon, managed to continue, while others, including Groundwell (with 11 taxpayers in 1377) and Moredon (with 16) came near to extinction. Mannington survived until the late fifteenth century, but was then deserted, and its cornfields were converted to sheep pasture. Grassy mounds denoted the position of the villagers' dwellings, and corrugations of ridge and furrow in the fields marked their acre strips of arable, until everything disappeared beneath the onslaught of West Swindon during the 1980s. Another community, which farmed part of Wroughton's claylands below Okus, is currently represented only by the protected earthworks and boundary banks of a former village street running from Westleaze to Westleaze Farm. It was known as Westlecot in the middle ages, and the new village built just to the east of it since 2006 has taken for itself an older form of its name, Wichelstowe.

The parish of Swindon in the middle ages was divided between five manors, and each appears to have had its own farming regime. On

Westleaze deserted hamlet seen from the air, revealing the earthworks of property boundaries ranged along a street. The site lies south of Swindon, between Okus and the motorway, next to the modern Wichel developments.

An estate map dated 1763 of Goddard property to the south and west of Old Swindon, showing enclosed fields in the Westlecot, Okus and Tismeads area, around Swindon Field, the area of open (or former open) arable cultivation. Much of this was quarried and now forms the Town Gardens. (WSA, 4179/1).

the southern and eastern edges of the parish were the small manors of Broome and Walcot, and occupying Swindon Hill itself and its southern slope was the most productive of the estates, known as High or West Swindon. It included a very large arable field on the hilltop, which was later exploited also by the quarries, together with pasture grounds on the hillside. The two remaining manors, known as East Swindon and Nethercott (which included Eastcott and Westcott) consisted largely of clayland, but each extended some distance up Swindon Hill, on the north and east sides, to benefit from the lighter, more easily worked soils.

Both these poorer, sparsely populated manors attempted to grow crops during the middle ages in open fields on the unsympathetic clay soil of the valley; but during the seventeenth century they converted much of their land to enclosed pasture. The enclosure in 1657 of Eastcott manor (as Nethercott had by this time become known) was the subject of a long legal agreement between the various freeholders. This begins by reciting the various difficulties which the farmers were facing. It tells us that the grounds and premises, 'had for a long time past remained much impoverished and decayed by reason of the unaptness of the tillable grounds for corne and grain, which were more apt for grass and hay'. The disorders and inconveniences of the existing regime, it continues, 'could not heretofore be reformed by the reason of the disagreement and wilfulness of some of the inhabitants and occupiers of land there, and by reason of the diversities of tenures and estates, and the said grounds and premises so lying open and dispersed'. Accordingly the old common fields and meadows were divided up, and allotted in blocks to the various freeholders. This process of enclosure imprinted on the landscape many of the lines which, two centuries later, would constrain and be respected by the brand new streets and terraces of New Swindon.

The first Ordnance Survey map of the Swindon area (overleaf), published in 1828, depicts a world far removed from that of fifty or a hundred years later. From the little foursquare hilltop town westwards to Lydiard, northwards to Blunsdon and eastwards to Wanborough stretched mile after mile of flat countryside, traversed by meandering streams and wandering lanes, and punctuated only by occasional isolated farms. Their venerably ancient names – Westcott, Penhill, Toothill, Walcot, Nythe – are entirely familiar to present-day Swindonians, but their surroundings are not. This older Swindon landscape has been almost completely forgotten, yet it underpins the entire structure and layout of the modern town and its suburbs.

The first edition Ordnance Survey map of the Swindon are

SWINDON LANDSCAPES

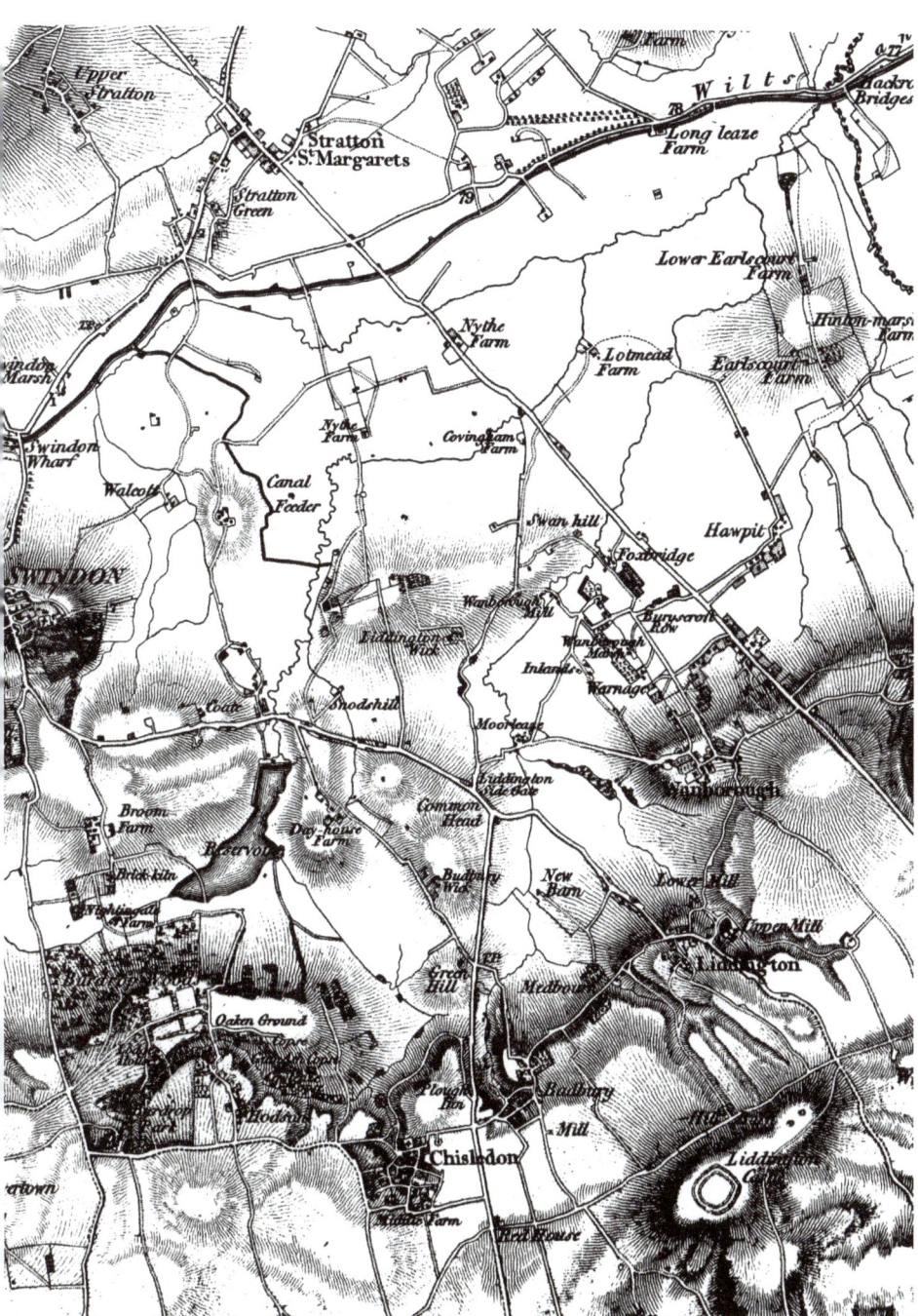

surveyed in 1815-16 and published in 1828

This elegant Regency terrace at the beginning of Bath Road was built around 1835, a few years after John Britton praised Swindon's sophistication, and just before the railway arrived to transform everything.

2
BUT A SMALL PLACE

Swindon is a market town, placed on an eminence, which affords an extensive prospect over some parts of Gloucestershire and Berkshire. The pleasantness of its situation, combined with other circumstances, have induced many persons of independent fortune to fix their residence at Swindon; and their mansions contribute as much to ornament the town as their social intercourse may be said to animate and enliven it. To this may be attributed, perhaps, that liberality of mind which now appears to characterise the inhabitants of this little town.

SO WROTE the topographer and antiquary John Britton, in part of his work about the 'beauties' of Wiltshire, which was published in 1825. By Swindon, of course, he meant Old Swindon – New Swindon did not then exist – and it is the evolution of settlement on Swindon Hill leading up to this plateau of Regency decorum which concerns us in the present chapter.

Stray finds of prehistoric artefacts, as well as archaeological work prior to new building, are developing a picture of intermittent human settlement on the hill from the time of nomadic mesolithic hunters and foragers through to the period of Roman colonization from *Durocornovium*. But prehistoric evidence here, generally in the form of flintwork, pits and burials, is really no more than might be expected on any tract of open, fertile, well drained and defensible land such as the hill during prehistory is presumed to have been.

Nor is it any surprise to find that astute Roman farmers and villa-owners also settled here – it would be more surprising if they did not. Over a century ago, in 1897, a local antiquary, Arthur Passmore, excavated part of what was probably a villa in the Okus area, and a

These neolithic artefacts – a polished stone axe, flint tools and a sherd of pottery – were found during excavations in 1977 behind Lloyd's Bank in High Street (Bernard Phillips).

few years later, in 1906, he also found evidence of a Roman building on the northern slope of the hill in what is now Queen's Park. Roman wells, ditches and building materials have subsequently been uncovered between Broome Manor and Coate. A fourth area of Roman activity on the hill, parts of which were excavated in 1975-6 and 1994, is perhaps the most important, because the site, a short distance due east of Old Swindon's market square around Dammas Lane, has yielded evidence from both earlier and later periods, as well as two phases of Roman buildings. The second Roman phase consisted of a rough stone-built structure, which could be dated from pottery and coins to the fourth century, not long before the breakdown of Roman rule. It replaced an earlier timber building on the site, and was in turn replaced by two small early Saxon huts.

These modest structures are perhaps the links in a chain which connects Roman *Durocornovium* with medieval Swindon and modern Old Town. We know that the community centred on *Durocornovium* was quarrying stone from Swindon Hill for some of its buildings, and there appears to have been a road leading up to the quarries from the

Roman town. We have also seen that *Durocornovium's* low-lying position, dictated by the junction of the Roman roads, was far from ideal. Damp and flooding were clearly troubling the inhabitants, as some buildings there were raised above ground level, rather like granaries on staddle stones, and the problem may have been made worse by a deteriorating climate at the end of the Roman period. It has been suggested that the late-Roman and early-Saxon discoveries at Old Town perhaps represent a shift away from *Durocornovium* to a more viable site on the hill.

Not far away from where the Roman building had been buried a much larger Saxon hut, nearly nine metres long, was discovered. Its walls had been constructed of wattle and daub, and much of the daub, preserving the impression of the woven wattle structure, had survived the fire which ended the building's career during the middle-Saxon period. Beneath the daub were some of the hut's contents, including a shelf of pots and the remains of a loom and other weaving equipment. Like other Saxon huts discovered nearby its floor was below ground level, a characteristic of buildings of the sixth and seventh centuries. Another excavation carried out in 1977 behind Lloyd's Bank in Swindon High Street uncovered the

From the remains of one of the Saxon huts excavated near the market place between 1975 and 1977 came clothmaking implements, including loom weights, shears, a comb and pins (Bernard Phillips).

Abandoned in 1852, with only its chancel and nave arcade remaining, Swindon's medieval Holy Rood church probably overlay an earlier building which stood at the heart of the late Saxon and Norman village, preceding the creation of the town in the thirteenth century.

same sequence of late-prehistoric and Roman settlement beneath a Saxon sunken hut, which had also been used for clothmaking.

Thus some kind of Saxon hamlet or village existed close to the centre of the later Swindon. The large weaving hut had later buildings superimposed upon it, which dated from the late-Saxon and early-medieval periods. But their alignment seemed to bear no relationship to the modern street plan. Indeed, more recent investigation detected a possible east–west street running across the line of the later High Street. It is probable, therefore, that between the middle-Saxon period and the twelfth or thirteenth century either there was a break in occupation or else a wholesale reorganisation of the settlement took place.

A likely context for any reorganisation of Swindon would have been an attempt to establish a market in about 1260, and so to turn the existing village into a small town. The archaeology so far described suggests that the earlier settlement may have been located to the east of the present High Street. Another clue to its position may be provided by the ruined church of Holy Rood next to the scant remains of the Goddard family's mansion now known as The Lawn, and close to the site of a mill. Although by all accounts an undistinguished building, the church was said to have incorporated a Norman column; this, together with a twelfth-century reference to a church at Swindon, suggests that it existed long before the market was set up. The mill is thought to have been the successor of one of the two at Swindon recorded in Domesday Book, and The Lawn is believed to occupy the site of its medieval predecessor. Their position therefore, some 300 metres east of Swindon High Street, tends to confirm the archaeological testimony.

If all these suppositions are correct then the present street layout of Old Town is likely to have been a planned addition tacked on to the western edge of an already existing village. Certainly the long, narrow strips known as burgage tenements running back from High Street and

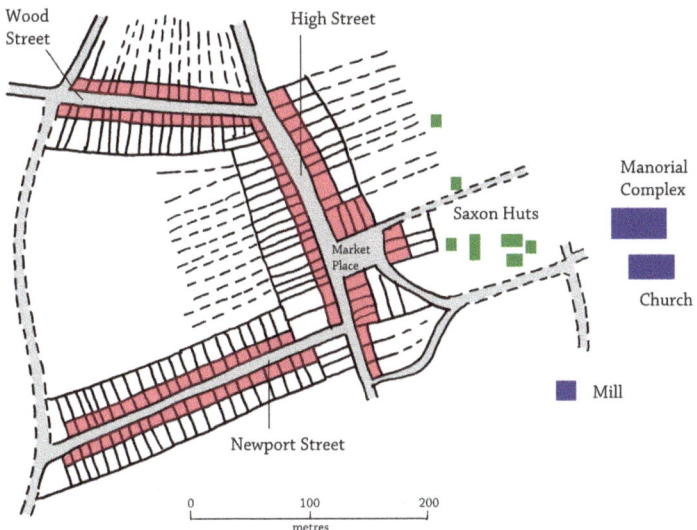

In the absence of property deeds and other records which might help to establish the medieval town's layout and extent, this is very much a conjectural interpretation of its possible thirteenth-century plan, and is based largely on much later property boundaries. Houses with their yards and narrow backlands probably lined High Street, Wood Street and Newport Street, and clustered round the modest market place. The earlier Saxon (green) and Norman (blue) settlements lay somewhat further east.

Wood Street suggest deliberate planning, and the expansionist mid-thirteenth century was exactly the right time for such a development. Similar urban extensions to existing villages occurred in many parts of England, and were common in Wiltshire between about 1210 and 1260. Sherston, Lacock and Market Lavington, to name but three, acquired markets and burgage tenure at this time.

Many so-called towns created in this way never developed into proper towns in the modern sense, and their medieval status could more accurately be described as that of urban villages. Indeed the three Wiltshire examples chosen have all been regarded for centuries just as large villages. In precisely the same way the medieval town of Swindon must not be overestimated.

The evidence for its urban career is remarkably slight. It seems not to have acquired a proper market charter during the middle ages and, were it not for a complaint by Marlborough tradesmen in 1274 that they had been suffering competition during the fifteen years past from an unofficial market in Swindon, we should have no idea when it began. There are, it is true, occasional references in medieval documents to a market and to burgages; there is by 1346 the appearance of the name Newport Street ('newport' means 'the new market'); and from 1289 Swindon was sometimes called 'Chipping' or 'Market Swindon'. An excavation in 1988 uncovered evidence of a possible boundary wall and wooden building in use in the fourteenth century on the corner of Devizes Road and Britannia Place; this is the first indication to be discovered that the town's built-up area extended so far westwards.

This modern passage-way follows the edge of a medieval burgage plot running back at right angles from Wood Street, which can be seen through the gap in the distance.

But the total absence of information about market trading and organization until the seventeenth century, the failure to secure a market charter until 1626, or to develop any kind of guild or corporate government –

BUT A SMALL PLACE

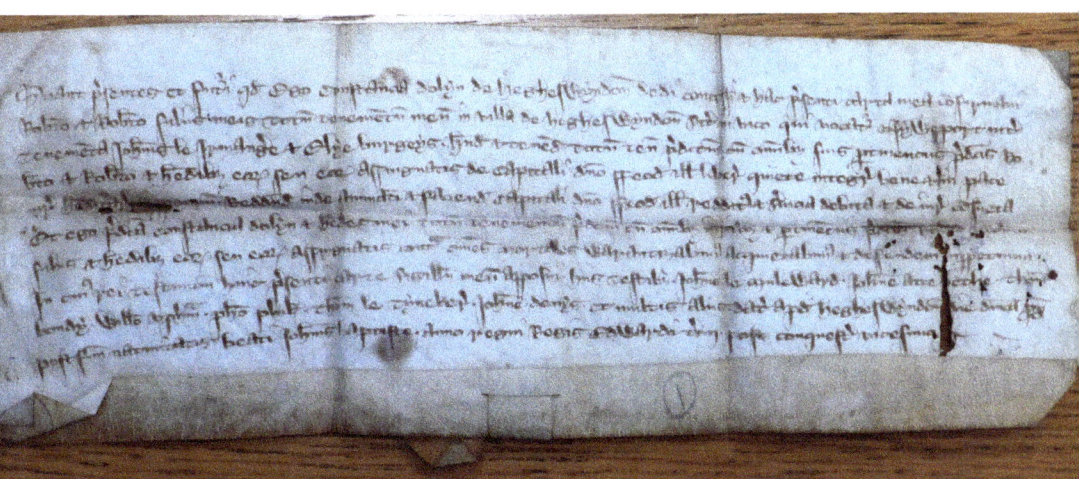

Although medieval Swindon figures frequently in the administrative and legal archives of central government, very few documents produced locally about property transactions or day-to-day working life appear to have survived – as they do for most towns and many villages. This deed is a rare exception. It is written mostly in Latin, but it takes a common form of documents of this period. The first line explains that Constance Dolyn of High Swindon (Hegheswyndon) has conveyed in fee simple (in other words, without any conditions) to her two sons, both called Robert (their names start the second line), all her tenement in the settlement called High Swindon in the street called Newport (Nyweport) between (on to the third line now) the tenements of John the ironmonger and Elye Burgeys. Next come several lines of legal verbiage standard for this kind of deed, followed by seven named witnesses. Then it takes more than the whole of the last line to tell us the date of the transaction, which took place at High Swindon on the Sunday after the feast of the birth of John the Baptist in the 20th year of King Edward III – or 3 September 1346 to put it more succinctly. Two years later the Black Death struck England, and we shall never know how many of Constance's family, and those of her seven witnesses, managed to survive the dreadful pandemic. (WSA, 1461/1).

all are indications that medieval Swindon remained essentially a larger-than-average agricultural community, with perhaps a little quarrying as a sideline, and possibly a few more tradesmen and specialist craftsmen than its neighbours, but that its career as a town had scarcely begun.

Writing in the 1670s John Aubrey, the Wiltshire intellectual, attributed a rise in Swindon's fortunes during the previous thirty or so years to two factors, its market and its quarries. The market, he explained, had benefited from outbreaks of plague before, and probably after, the civil war. These disrupted normal marketing, and frightened

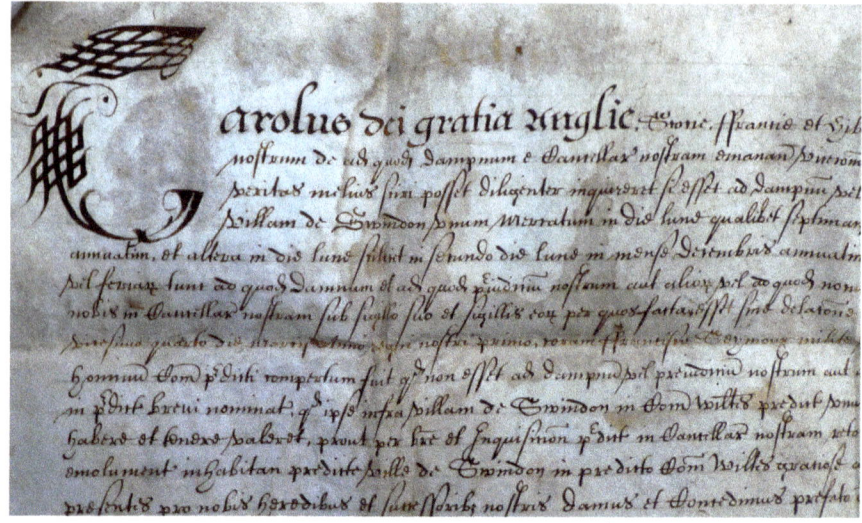

The initial capital (C for Carolus, i.e. Charles I) and the first part of a copy of the 1626 charter granting to Thomas Goddard the right to hold a weekly Monday market (unum mercatum in die lune) and two annual fairs in Swindon. By this date the market and fairs had been held, at least intermittently, for more than three centuries, so this document was ratification of a fait accompli. *(WSA, 1461/15).*

cattle-dealers away from their usual centre at Highworth, some 10km to the north-east. Swindon, with its Monday market recently placed on a new and legitimate footing by the 1626 royal charter, appears to have taken and retained some of Highworth's trade. The civil wars, too, were bad for Highworth. The town was garrisoned by royalist soldiers, who appear to have intimidated local graziers attending the market; in consequence they moved their business to Swindon.

Aubrey also claimed that the Purbeck limestone, for which the town had become famous by the time that he was writing, was discovered in about 1640, only five feet below ground. Stone from Swindon Hill had been exploited, as we have seen, in Roman times, and doubtless supplied local needs during the middle ages. There is a reference to stone slates being taken from Swindon to Sevenhampton in 1301, and an old quarry is referred to in deeds from 1641. But it was during the seventeenth century that Swindon stone acquired a reputation, not only for its smoothness and whiteness when used internally, but also for its resistance to damp. It was in demand during the rebuilding of London after the fire in 1666, and Aubrey implies that carriage was overland to Lechlade and then down the Thames. Certainly quarrymen begin to figure in Swindon manorial records from about 1670, both when they wished to purchase leases of lands for quarrying, and when they fell foul of authority for leaving excavations unfenced, to the danger of travellers.

Active and former quarries along the ridge to the west of Old Town, mapped by the Ordnance Survey in 1886. Much of the area shown was landscaped to become the Town Gardens a few years later, in 1894.

The Town Gardens, beautifully maintained, exhibit many changes of level, the result of quarrying, but also include works of public art, an aviary, refreshment kiosk and this elegant bandstand, which dates from 1936.

Aubrey's impression of Swindon as a community on the increase during the seventeenth century is undoubtedly correct, and other sources of information help us to quantify its progress. During the eighty years prior to 1640 the new owners of High Swindon, the Goddard family, appear to have made only very modest progress. In 1563 their estate included 60 houses and 40 cottages; by 1640 this housing stock had increased by a mere 8, suggesting a rough total population on their manor at both dates of 400-450. During the 1640s there were at least 30 families on the other main Swindon manor, Eastcott, and probably a few others at Walcot and Broome, so we should perhaps add 150-200 to give an approximate total population of Swindon parish of 550-650. The principal Swindon manor more than two centuries earlier, in 1377, claimed 248 adult taxpayers, and this, after allowing for children and tax evaders, might also yield a total population of 400-450. Another 88 taxpayers (perhaps representing 150 inhabitants) lived elsewhere in the parish in 1377, suggesting a total in the range 550-600. These calculations, like most historical statistics, are fraught with uncertainty, but they do offer a superficial impression of stability or stagnation. One other figure, a claim in 1627 that 9 alehouses were too many for an adult population of fewer than 300, is perhaps an underestimate in order to strengthen an argument, but even if true would multiply up to a total population approaching 500, not far below our estimate.

Two further statistics bring the story down to Aubrey's old age. In 1676 a religious census returned 580 (adult) communicants in Swindon, which would suggest a total population of about 900. In 1697, the year of Aubrey's death, a list was made of the names of all Swindon's inhabitants. The manuscript was saved from burning by a Cirencester gentleman during the nineteenth century, and is now a little damaged, but it seems to yield a total of 795 names (791 and 808 are other people's computations). So we may be seeing a rise from 550-650 in 1640, to 800-900 by the end of the century, and Aubrey's testimony appears quite credible. A further modest rise occurred during the eighteenth century, as by 1801 the population had almost reached 1,200.

But before we tackle the eighteenth century, the 1697 list deserves a second glance. Not only does it list everyone's names, but it also assigns an occupation to each householder. Thomas Goddard, who had been lord of the principal manor for nearly fifty years, heads the list, followed by members of the Vilett family, owners of the clayland manor of Eastcott, and Henry Thompson, vicar since 1663. We know, incidentally, from another source that the vicar was forever running into debt, and borrowing money from Goddard. Five other families are listed as having independent means, and there were fifteen yeoman families, accounting for some 7-8% of the total population.

The largest group, nearly one-quarter of the total, was made up of labourers and their families, but there were also significant numbers of textile workers – weavers, tailors and drapers – and masons (most of them quarrymen, no doubt), together accounting for about one-sixth of the workforce. The list includes most of the trades – such as bakers, coopers, saddlers, shoemakers, barbers, butchers and carpenters – which we might expect to find in any small town of the period, as well as one or two more exotic specialists. There is a tobacco cutter and a 'translator' (probably a cobbler who concentrated on renovating old shoes), a combmaker and a cheese factor.

The existence of five or six inns and an alehouse implies that, although Swindon did not lie on a major road and so could not benefit much from passing trade, nevertheless the vigour of its market and quarrying industry was considerable. A survey in 1686 found that the town's inns could accommodate a total of 14 travellers and no fewer than 91 horses; perhaps they were geared to catering for long-distance waggoners with their teams.

The Goddard Arms, Old Swindon's principal inn. The present impressive long façade fronting High Street dates from about 1815, but an inn has stood here since the seventeenth century.

From a medieval urban village, therefore, Swindon graduated during the seventeenth century to the status of a small country town. It was a workaday place of tradesmen and labourers, and it had not yet developed the air of polite society which it exuded after 1800. It was still of less consequence than the neighbouring towns of Highworth and Wootton Bassett, and much less important than Cricklade and Marlborough. And it could still suffer put-downs. In 1731

Square House, a fine Georgian building of about 1770 looking down on the market place.

a topographical writer sniffily remarked: 'It is so inconsiderable a place, that our histories take no notice of it'. As late as the 1790s a directory introduced Swindon as, 'but a small place, though the houses are well built, and of stone'.

Eighteenth-century Swindon, as depicted on maps of 1763 and 1773, consisted of three principal streets, forming three sides of a square. High Street continued southwards as Lower Town and northwards as Brookwell Hill or Brock Hill (present-day Cricklade

Swindon's second manor house, 42 Cricklade Street, built by and belonging to the Vilett family, dates from 1729. It is widely regarded as the finest town house in Swindon, and one of the best in Wiltshire. In poor condition for many years, it has been carefully renovated.

This detail from a 1763 Goddard estate map (re-orientated so that north is at the top) gives us the earliest surviving street plan of the town. The market place and the three principal streets of the town are shown, as is the road, here called Brookwell Hill (now Cricklade Street) leading down to the Drove. The mansion house and church are shown, and property belonging to the Goddards is distinguished by letters of the alphabet. As was usual with estate maps, the cartographer has not included the many houses and other buildings and land that did not belong to the client. (WSA, 4179/1).

Street), a much steeper descent than now and the scene of a fatal coaching accident. The market square, opening off High Street, included in its centre a small circular building, presumably of wood, which housed the pillory and stocks, and was used by traders as a shelter. It may have been, or have replaced, the market cross referred to in 1662; it was in poor condition in 1750, and was demolished in 1793 using chains and a team of horses.

Opposite the square, along the western side of High Street to the junction with Wood Street, a number of eighteenth-century and earlier buildings have survived. The Bell Hotel retains work which may be of 1515, and other houses range in date from 1631 to the late-eighteenth century. At the beginning of Cricklade Street, beyond the Goddard Arms, is a building which was described by Sir John Betjeman as 'one of the most distinguished town houses in Wiltshire'. No.42 Cricklade Street was built in 1729, and became the home of the Vilett family, who owned Eastcott manor. Its architecture of local stone and brick marries the two foundations on which Swindon is built, the limestone of Swindon Hill, and the clay of the vale. For some years until the early 2000s it was left in poor condition, but is now restored (as apartments) to former opulence, lording itself over the steep hill and poking fun at passers-by with its cheeky keystones above the windows.

Two of Mr Vilett's scary keystones confronting passers-by from the façade of 42 Cricklade Street.

Wood Street, which runs west from High Street, is first recorded by name in 1599, and is so called on the map (opposite) of 1763. The name presumably refers, like its namesake in Wootton Bassett, to the fact that it leads towards Braydon Forest. But it also had two more colloquial names, Blacksmith's Street and Windmill Street, both because of premises adjoining it. It was remembered as a street of mean thatched cottages, and this poorer quarter continued down the hill along the lane

The King's Arms Hotel, expensive high Victorian of 1869, epitomises Old Town's 'window of opportunity' to garner wealth, after the railway and its working families had arrived but before New Swindon's shopping and other facilities had been fully established to cater for them. Wood Street still resonates an air of this prosperity.

known as Little London. Wood Street's present commercial character is largely Victorian, and results from the period when Old Swindon traders catered also for the needs of the burgeoning new railway town.

Newport Street, the third side of the square, runs at right angles from the southern end of High Street, and, like Wood Street, it had an alternative name. To old men in the nineteenth century it was always Bull Street, and was regarded as rather an eyesore. William Morris, whom we shall encounter in the next chapter, explained its derivation and character thus:

> The *Bull* was a low, thatched, cottage looking building, very much like most of the other houses on the street. Indeed, if the houses on the street were not remarkable for their uniformity, it was owing to their all having been put up according to some rule of thumb . . . In a word, the architecture of the street may be described as that of the Squatters – of men who, by some means or other, became possessed of a bit of land, and built themselves a house thereon with such materials as came readiest to hand.

From this description it sounds very much as if Newport Street, after the planned medieval town had failed to develop, reverted to being a country lane, and was only built up again in the seventeenth century, by informal squatting when the town's population began to grow. Short Hedge, as the fourth side of the square of roads was known (now Devizes Road), remained in an undeveloped state until the nineteenth century.

Newport Street, the oldest recorded street in Swindon, and probably a key element in the thirteenth-century town plan, seems to have become impoverished later in its career. All these cottages have long been demolished, to be replaced by offices and a car park. (WSHC, P18143).

The bases of Swindon's economy, the market and the quarries, appear to have continued throughout the eighteenth century. A regular trade by stage waggon developed with London, carrying meat, cheese and other dairy products to the capital from its depot on the site of the later Town Hall or corn exchange. There are dark hints too about another, clandestine, trade, in smuggled spirits brought ashore along the south coast, and concealed in the cellars of Swindon houses.

The town's character was set, and local government controlled, by its forceful leading family, the Goddards. Despite repeated disputes with the vicar over tithes, which spilled over into litigation in 1777, the Goddards were no friends of nonconformity either. Pleydell Goddard in

1741 orchestrated a savage persecution against an itinerant evangelist, John Cennick, and his followers when he tried to preach in the town. According to Cennick's diary guns, halberds and a fire engine spraying ditchwater were all turned on them to intimidate and inflict injury, while Goddard, 'sat on horseback the whole time, laughing to see us so treated'. Such anatagonism was not uncommon, but it is eloquent testimony to the power wielded by the lords of the manor that nonconformity made virtually no impact in Swindon until after 1800, even though quarrymen elsewhere were generally staunch dissenters.

This ugly episode in 1741 was still remembered when John Britton was writing eighty years later, and he contrasted such prejudice with the liberality of the Swindonians he encountered. One indication of a small measure of enlightenment dawning on the town was a free school, established in Newport Street in 1764. It was administered by a trust, and its instigator and driving force (to give him his due) was Thomas Goddard, lord of the manor. The curriculum included the three 'R's and religious instruction according to Anglican principles; the teaching of science and foreign languages was not permitted.

A generation later, in 1804, an Independent chapel and dissenting academy opened, also in Newport Street. Thomas and James Strange, members of a leading Swindon family of bankers and tradesmen, sponsored the venture, and the first pastor/schoolmaster was a certain George Mantell, 'a fair scholar'. But his story, and that of his nephew, Gideon Mantell, belong to the next chapter.

3
THE FIRST PUSH

GIDEON MANTELL spent the year 1804 in Swindon, as his uncle's pupil at the new dissenting academy in Newport Street. His home was in Sussex, but he had studied under George Mantell since 1801, and moved with him to Swindon from Westbury, where he had been an Independent pastor. George remained at Swindon until his death in 1832, building up the congregation and reputation of the Newport Street chapel, and running his school for as many as eighteen pupils at a time. Gideon stayed in Swindon little more than a year, before returning to Lewes to embark on a medical career. But it was as a geologist and palaeontologist that he made his name, and to him is credited the discovery and first description of several dinosaur species. In later life,

The independent (Congregational) chapel in Newport Street was new when George Mantell became its first pastor in 1804. It continued in use until 1866 (Large).

according to his diary, he paid four nostalgic visits to the town, in 1827, 1832, 1841 and 1846. He died in 1852.

Mantell's life spanned the most important period in Swindon's history. His schoolday memories, of reading poetry in the shade of the schoolhouse eaves, strolling in the 'Long Walk' (part of The Lawn) with his adolescent first love (who was a daughter of the prominent Strange family), and collecting in the quarries the first of the fossils which would shape his life – these were Regency recollections of the genteel country town which John Britton has already described to us. They are paralleled by the school bills of a young lady, Miss Betty Wheeler, who was being educated at Swindon between 1796 and 1800. Expenses included writing-books, dancing, shoes and gloves, a servant, a trimmed bonnet, sash and umbrella, a 'filligree caddy', and various items of haberdashery, including 8s 8d (£0.43p, slightly more than a labourer's weekly wage) spent on cord for her stays.

Mantell's first return visit, shortly after the former Miss Strange's death, was accomplished by stagecoach as far as Marlborough, and then by post-chaise (a kind of private hire coach). And his second visit, in 1832, was only a brief stop while travelling by coach from Oxford to Bristol. But in July 1841 he was able to travel down from London, purely as a day's excursion. He started at ten, he tells us, from the Great Western Railroad at Paddington, and arrived at the Swindon station at one, from where he walked through the fields to the town. He visited scenes of his youth, but spent most time at the quarries collecting specimens. At six he walked back through the fields to the railway station, accompanied by a quarryman who carried his heavy load of fossils, to catch the seven o'clock train back to London. His last nostalgic return, in 1846, was partly to meet up with his son, a young civil engineer who was working for Brunel on new railway lines in Wiltshire.

Paradoxically, it was during Mantell's idyllic year at Swindon, 1804, that the remote hilltop town took a large step closer to the outside world. Canals were an accompaniment to the industrializing Midlands and North, and came comparatively late to the South. Nevertheless the linking of London and Bristol by water had been proposed as early as the sixteenth century, and various schemes to marry the Bristol Avon and the Thames by canal were strenuously advocated by John Aubrey in the seventeenth. One of these was planned to extend from Malmesbury on

This map shows the principal canals that crossed southern England in the early nineteenth century. The Wilts and Berks, and its branch, the North Wilts (both here marked in red), by linking rivers and other canals, offered a through route between Bristol and London for three decades before the railway arrived. Its impact on Swindon and its neighbourhood was enormous, not only in stimulating trade at the time, but also on the subsequent layout of the railway town. Its presence was also one of the factors that influenced the railway company to site its works here.

the Avon to Wootton Bassett, heading presumably for the River Ray (a tributary of the Thames) west of Swindon. But as with most of Aubrey's ingenious projects, it came to nothing.

Renewed interest during the 1790s led to the construction of two canals across north Wiltshire in order to achieve the union of Avon and Thames, Bristol and London. The Kennet and Avon Canal took the southerly route, through Devizes, the Vale of Pewsey and the Kennet Valley. Branching from it, at Semington near Melksham, the Wilts and Berks Canal struck north and then east, through Dauntsey Vale to Swindon and the Vale of White Horse.

From Chaddington near Wootton Bassett to South Marston the canal maintained a level course across the claylands north of Swindon Hill. This stretch was the highest point, or summit, of the navigation, and construction was carried out from west to east between 1802 and 1805. A wharf was built below Swindon, and this was in use by March 1804. The canal was completed along its whole length in 1810,

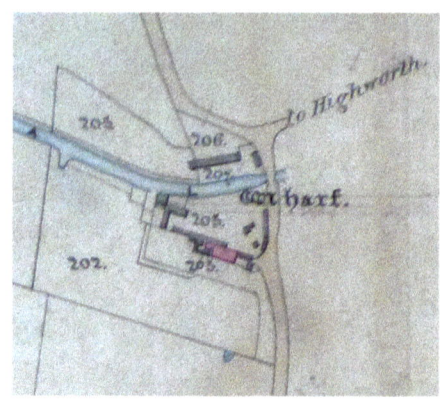

A wharf was built on the canal to serve the hilltop town, and a house (in pink) and various outbuildings (in grey) are shown on the Swindon tithe map of about 1840. The canal was bridged here to serve the road (now Drove Road) leading down from the town towards Cricklade (now County Road). The site of the wharf therefore is now occupied by the Magic Roundabout and adjacent fire station (WSA, T/A Swindon).

and immediately plans were laid to connect it to another canal, the Thames and Severn, which ran through Stroud to Lechlade. The route of the linking canal, which came to be known as the North Wilts, was decided in 1812. It left the Wilts and Berks near Eastcott (at the heart of modern-day Swindon) and ran north to meet the Thames and Severn at Latton. After much prevarication it was completed in 1819. Finally

Detail from a map of the proposed North Wilts Canal showing the link with other waterways (Wilts. Museum, DZSWS:MSS.2522).

Proposed North Wilts Canal.

THIS Canal, by uniting the Thames and Severn Canal with the Wilts and Berks, will complete a Communication between the two great Rivers, the Severn and the Thames, and be the shortest, cheapest, and most expeditious Line of Conveyance for the fine Navy Timber and valuable Products of the Forest of Dean, and the Manufactures and Merchandize of South Wales, Gloucestershire, Herefordshire, and the north west parts of the Kingdom, to the Metropolis.

To obtain so desirable a Communication, Parliament in 1783 sanctioned the making the Thames and Severn Canal, and the Proprietors expended upon it upwards of two hundred and fifty thousand pounds: but the public object has been defeated by the continued bad state of the Navigation of the River, between Lechlade and Oxford; and from the same cause the Proprietors are suffering a very serious loss and injury.

The proposed Canal is about eight miles in length, and will not only avoid the bad part of the River, but shorten the distance twenty miles.

It will add greatly to the general Trade of the Thames with the Metropolis; for what it will take from the River between Lechlade and Abingdon, it will restore to it at the latter place with a vast increase, which will be insured by so improved and shortened a Navigation; and it is totally free from all objection with respect to any diversion of Streams flowing to the Thames.

A more particular account, with a Plan of the Canal and Rivers, has been sent to every Member of the House of Commons; and the Promoters, relying upon the merits of their Case, hope for your attendance at the Second Reading of the Bill, on Monday next the 5th of April, at Four o'Clock.

Tyler, Printer,
Rathbone Place.

Part of the Case of the Promoters of the North Wilts Canal, presented in 1813 (Wilts. Museum, DZSWS:MSS.2522).

Canals generally have a 'summit', the highest stretch of water from which traffic descends by locks to connect with towns and rivers at lower levels, and in many places it proved necessary to keep the water level topped up by a reservoir. Swindon is the summit of the Wilts and Berks, and Coate Water was constructed in 1821-2 to be its reservoir. It was later the fictionalised setting for the waterborne adventures of Bevis, the child hero created by Richard Jefferies, and has at least since the 1870s been a favourite leisure destination for Swindonians - and a nature reserve since 1975. The diving stage dates from 1935.

Coate Reservoir, to the east of Swindon, was built in 1821-2 in order to overcome chronic water shortages at the canal summit.

Looking back across more than fifty years of hindsight two local newspapermen, the old William Morris and the young Richard Jefferies, both saw the seeds of New Swindon in the arrival of the canal. It was 'the first push', according to Jefferies. Morris went further: 'It was not only the greatest public work that had ever been undertaken in this part of the country, but the revolution it was to effect, and the impetus it was to give to trade, was simply marvellous.' More recent historians have tended to understate its importance, inexplicably in my view. For just as (for me) the key to decoding outer Swindon lies in the Roman roads, medieval farms and enclosure of the land beneath the modern suburbs, so the canal (more even than the railway) unlocks the puzzles of central Swindon.

At the time the canal's effect was fourfold. First, and of greatest immediate interest to the residents of Swindon, it led to a spectacular reduction in the price of fuel. Coal from the Somerset collieries (and after the North Wilts Canal was built from the Forest of Dean as well) was the main commodity carried along the canal, and local people came to rely on the cheap and plentiful supply to such an extent that, if in winter the water froze over and the barges were stopped, enterprising local farmers took waggons to the coalfield in order to make good the deficiency.

The second consequence of the canal was to stimulate the general trade of the area, by dispelling Swindon's rather aloof reputation, often repeated, as being a town which lay aside from main lines of communication. The canal opened up Swindon's agricultural hinterland, which in turn encouraged its market, and enabled it to increase its population in line with neighbouring towns and villages. Swindon's main producers of the period, however, its stone quarriers, appear not to have exploited to any great extent the possibility of cheaper and easier transport for their product which the canal offered. This may perhaps be attributable to the hostility of William Dunsford, the canal's superintendent from 1817 to 1839. Dunsford seems to have had extensive business interests 'on the side', which he tried to protect from competition, including a quarry producing Bath stone at Monkton Farleigh in west Wiltshire.

But the quarriers of Swindon did benefit from the canal in another way. During its construction (and long before Dunsford's arrival) they were called upon to supply large quantities of building and paving stone. Prodigious numbers of bricks, too, were made for the canal at temporary brickyards built close to the route. All this activity helped the local economy, which was further stimulated by the spending power of the itinerant navvies employed on building the canal. William Morris sarcastically commented on local people's supposed altruism regarding the navvies' welfare, 'especially so long as they had any money to spare, not of course for the purpose of getting it from them, but only to help them to take care of it, and see that it was not lost'(!).

But in addition to the effects which the canal had on Swindon at the time, there are two other reasons for emphasising its importance in the town's development. The first, which we shall consider shortly, is that its presence was one of the reasons expressed in 1840 for locating the

A detail from the Swindon tithe map of about 1840 showing the canals crossing what would become New Swindon, and the line of the railways then under construction. The much later Town Hall and Theatre Square will be built on the site of Upper Eastcott, from which a track then ran north-westwards (and would become Regent Street) to cross the canal by Golden Lion Bridge. The railway station will occupy much of plots 30-35 and the railway village plots 63-4. The field boundaries and canal bridges were fundamental to the layout of the new town (WSA, T/A Swindon).

THE FIRST PUSH

railway works at Swindon. The second is the profound effect it has had on the layout of New Swindon.

Prior to the 19th century, as we have seen, the boggy claylands north of Swindon Hill were very sparsely populated. Apart from Westcott and Eastcott Farms maps show nothing, and Britton reported that local people regarded one area, which they called 'quaving-gogs', as dangerous because of its deep quagmires. The building of the canal established a kind of base-line across the site of New Swindon which can still be clearly traced today. From the Cambria Bridge area it runs north-eastwards to become Canal Walk and The Parade, two of central Swindon's principal shopping streets; then its line is followed by Fleming Way to the 'Magic Roundabout', which is close to the site of Swindon Wharf. The railway, railway village, and Victorian housing in the Manchester Road area all owe their alignment to the canal. And because it was still very much in use while New Swindon developed and grew it acted as a barrier, so that anyone wishing to cross it had to use one of five bridges. These – Cambria Bridge, Milton Road Bridge, Golden Lion Bridge, Whale Bridge

The northern end of Commercial Road, created in 1890, was carried over the canal by this bridge, also known as Milton Road Bridge, and anyone venturing westward under it enters a different world. No longer the shopping mall and car parks - the line of the infilled canal is preserved behind the backyards of houses on either side, and leads uninterrupted to Cambria Bridge, and eventually to Rushy Platt, where the canal itself has been restored.

and Wharf Bridge – therefore functioned as benchmarks, dictating the northern ends of Commercial Road, Regent Street and Princes Street, and thus influencing the entire layout of the Victorian town.

But these are matters to think about later, and must wait until after we have considered the circumstances and consequences of a certain famous picnic. Between 1801 and 1841 Swindon's population (excluding the recently arrived railway workers and itinerant navvies) increased by over 60%, from 1,198 to 1,952. Highworth, Wroughton and Wootton Bassett all returned increases of the same order. Swindon, therefore, was developing in line with its neighbours. Their increase was rather higher than Wiltshire as a whole (40%), but not quite as high as the United Kingdom average (almost 70%) over the same period. As Sir John Betjeman remarked: 'Anyone wishing to see what Swindon would have looked like . . . [if the railway works had not come] has only to look

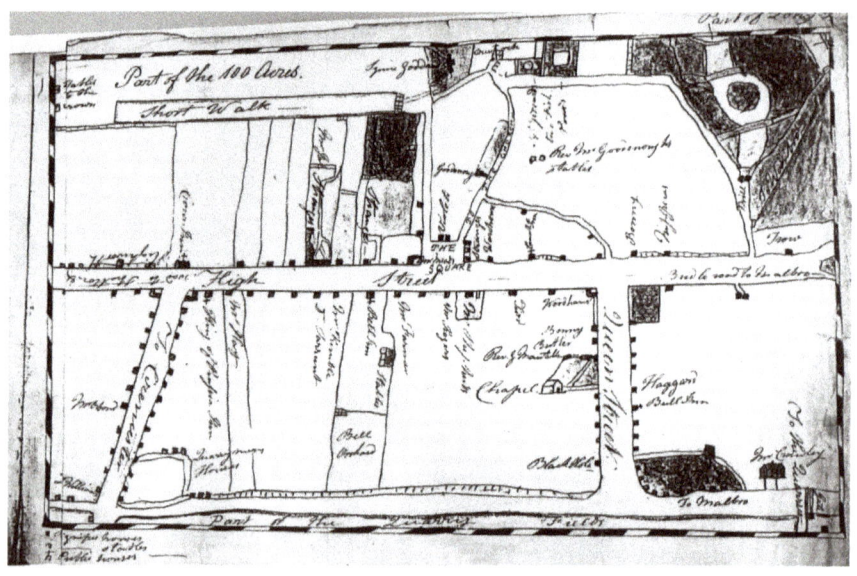

This interesting sketch map of Swindon in 1804 is preserved about as far away as is possible, in New Zealand's national archives. Drawn by Gideon Mantell while a pupil of his uncle, Revd. George Mantell (whose chapel is shown), it depicts most of the small town's significant buildings, and its three streets lined with houses. For Gideon the road to the quarries and the quarrymen's houses had particular significance, as it was in Swindon's quarries that he developed the interest in geology which was to become his profession. The map is drawn with north to the left (Nat. Lib. of New Zealand, Alexander Turnbull Library, fMS-Papers-0083-122).

at Highworth, once the chief town of this corner of Wiltshire'.

There were a few buildings at Swindon Wharf, including a gentleman's villa, 'surpassing the second, and approaching the first class', according to William Cobbett in 1826 – the gentleman in question was William Dunsford, the canal's entrepreneurial superintendent. But apart from the wharf, Swindon's 60% growth to 1841 was absorbed within the existing town on the hill.

Evidence of the prosperity and expansion of these years may still be seen at Old Town. As a schoolboy in 1804 Gideon Mantell drew a sketch map of Swindon, and this shows that Devizes Road (then known as Short Hedge or Horse Fair) was only built up at its northern end, where it joins Wood Street. Here six quarrymen's houses are depicted, three on the street, three set back along a lane. By 1818 Britannia Place had begun to be developed, and by 1841 there were twelve houses in Devizes Road itself. North of Wood Street, in Little London, was an area of poor houses, including a common lodging-house, and to the west developed the fashionable quarter of the town. Here, along Bath Road (then called The Sands) was built Apsley House, which until recently housed Swindon Museum, as well as the urbane brick terrace of town houses beyond, each with its cast-iron porch, and Prospect Place to the north, enjoying the open vista across the clay vale.

Apsley House on the corner of Bath Road dates from about 1835 and is a sign of Old Swindon's growing prosperity before the railway arrived. For many years the building housed the town's museum, but had closed when this photograph was taken in 2020.

That vista was not to remain unaltered for long. In July 1833 a young engineer, Isambard Kingdom Brunel, was appointed in Bristol by a company which in the following month adopted the name 'Great Western Railway'. Its aim was to link London, Bath and Bristol by rail. A route via Wootton Bassett and Wantage had been surveyed as early as 1824, and a similar line was recommended by Brunel in preference to the more southerly option, through the Vale of Pewsey. Parliamentary approval for the railway was secured in August 1835, and work began from both ends. This triggered residents of Bath's rival, Cheltenham, to petition for a connecting line from Swindon to Cheltenham, which was duly authorised in June 1836 as the Cheltenham and Great Western Union Railway. In December 1840 the railway from London reached Swindon, and a temporary station was built at Hay Lane, between Swindon and Wootton Bassett. In May 1841 the first leg of the Cheltenham line, as far as Cirencester, was completed, and in the following month Box Tunnel, the last and greatest obstacle on the line west to Bristol, was conquered, so that trains could begin to run between London and Bristol. Gideon Mantell, when he visited Swindon in July 1841 aboard the Bristol train, must therefore have been one of the first passengers. Swindon Junction Station, although in use from about May 1841, was not completed until July 1842, and the link with Cheltenham was finished in May 1845.

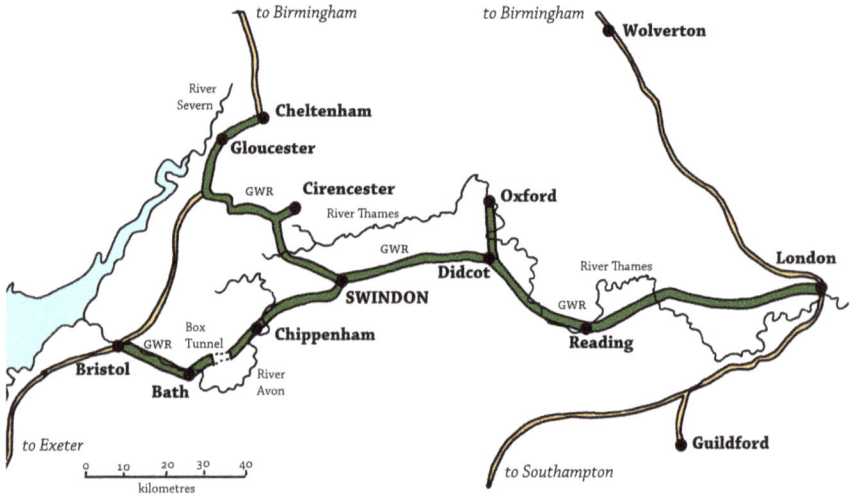

The first trunk and branch lines of the Great Western Railway, in green, and other early railways, in yellow.

It is no use trying to appreciate these bald but momentous statements, unless we are prepared to dispel from our minds our hindsight of all that was to follow, and to put ourselves into Mantell's shoes, as he made his way across the fields back to the station with his fossils in 1841. The railways planned and built in the 1830s were the direct result of two factors: the success of the Liverpool and Manchester Railway (opened in 1830) in showing that steam locomotion between cities was a viable and profitable undertaking; and the availability of capital (and willingness of its owners) to speculate in similar projects. Of the hundred or so railway companies sanctioned up to 1840 most were concerned with relatively short distances; indeed by 1844 only 2,000 miles of track had been laid. The Great Western scheme was among the most ambitious of the early schemes, and was paralleled only by the Grand Junction (Liverpool to Birmingham) and the London and Birmingham, both opened in 1838. For shareholders, directors, contractors and employees alike – let alone passengers – the enterprise was fraught with risk and uncertainty.

For the Wiltshire countryman the possibility of a railway provoked a mixture of responses. Some, like the old farmer recalled in an anecdote by William Morris, refused to countenance the existence of such a thing. On being told about it, he took the news as, 'a most wicked and deliberate attempt on the part of an old friend to deceive and mislead him,' and could not believe that there would ever be a mode of travel to surpass the yellow post-chaise which he had seen with his own eyes. Others, including many landowners, greeted the prospect with hostility, regarding it as an intrusion on the privacy of their estates, and an unwelcome move towards social equality. In engineering their routes, railway companies repeatedly bent to the demands of landed interests. In Swindon the lord of the manor, Ambrose Goddard, opposed a plan to build the line to the south of the canal, with a station at the foot of Drove Road, because it impinged on his parkland.

But such opposition was rarely fuelled by simple prejudice or inconvenience. Goddard, for example, as well as looking after his Swindon interests, was also from 1835 chairman of the Wilts and Berks Canal, whose fate was closely bound up with the new railway. Many local people watched the progress of the railway with interest, not as a potential threat but as a possible source of riches. In April 1836, before the Cheltenham branch was even ratified by Parliament, an advertisement appeared in Wiltshire newspapers advertising fields at Eastcott for sale. Because of their proximity to the proposed railway lines, and the likelihood that a railway depot would be built near them – if not actually on them – it was claimed that they had an 'incalculable' future value. As it turned out, of course, the advertisement was no exaggeration, and Richard Jefferies recalled that one or two fortunes were made out of land which hitherto had been scarcely worth the trouble of attending to, and covered with furze.

> **SWINDON, WILTS.**
> **A FREEHOLD ESTATE,**
> *(Bounded on the south side by the line of the " Great Western Railway," and on the west side by the line of the projected " Cheltenham and Great Western Union Railway," and the North Wilts Canal ;)*
>
> FOR Peremptory SALE by PUBLIC AUCTION, by W. DORE, (by order of Trustees), at the BELL INN, in *Swindon*, on MONDAY the 18th day of April, 1836, precisely at four o'clock in the afternoon, under conditions ; consisting of three Inclosures of very useful and productive Meadow or Pasture LAND, containing together by admeasurement 21A. 3R. 15P., lying in the tything of *Eastcott*, in the parish of Swindon, and now occupied by most respectable yearly tenants.
>
> This little Estate, independent of its locality, is desirable but when it is considered that both the above Railways will touch upon, or very near it, and that the important depot for the junction of the Cheltenham with the Great Western is not unlikely to be actually upon, and must be at all events very near this Property, its future value is incalculable. The speculator will rarely meet with such an opportunity of reaping profit at little risk. The Land Tax is redeemed, and it is divided into three Fields, and will be sold in two lots, as follows:
>
> | | A. | R. | P |
> |---|---|---|---|
> | Lot 1.—Loppos Hill Grounds, with useful Stalls thereon, contains | 12 | 3 | 32 |
> | York's Upper Breach | 6 | 3 | 16 |
> | Lot 2.—The Three Acres, formerly part of Loppos Hill | 2 | 0 | 7 |
> | Total | 21 | 3 | 15 |
>
> Part of the Purchase Money may remain on Mortgage, if required.
> For further information, apply to Messrs. CROWDY, Solicitors, Swindon.

If the prospect of becoming a railway junction was greeted with a mixture of prejudice, uncertainty and excited speculation, it was overshadowed in 1840 by an even more far-reaching proposal. Daniel Gooch, an ambitious engineer from Northumberland, was twenty years old when appointed Brunel's superintendent of locomotives in 1837. By 1840, with engines in service over much of the line and the prospect of completion to Bristol within months, Gooch was asked to recommend a site for a locomotive repair depot. There are hints in letters of the time of the company's, and Brunel's, indecision about this. A site near Bristol, or Reading, or Didcot, were all possibilities, and Brunel in 1840 was toying with developing Hay Lane, the line's temporary terminus near Wootton Bassett. But Gooch's recommendation was Swindon, and in a letter to Brunel on 13 September he set out some of his reasons.

Locomotives of the period were not considered capable of operating the entire distance from London to Bristol, and so a change would be necessary. Although Swindon was not halfway, it did lie at a transition, from the relatively flat and easy going tracks up the Thames Valley, to the shorter but more demanding descent through Box to

THE FIRST PUSH

The advertisement (opposite page) for an auction of farmland appeared in local newspapers in 1836. The agent was well aware of the potential value of a site adjacent to the new railway lines, and speculated that a depot would need to be built there, although no decision had been taken at this stage. From the description of the property and the names and acreages of the plots, it seems likely that the larger portion of Lot 1, Loppos Hill Grounds, is what on the tithe map is numbered 29 and 44, and the smaller portion, Yorks Upper Breach, may be 30, 31 and 32. The former portion was not built over with railway workshops until the 1870s, although by 1840 it belonged to the railway company; but the latter became the site of the junction station. Edward Ewer, a Cricklade farmer, owned 30, 31 and 32 in 1840, so he may have been the shrewd investor four years earlier who acquired the site of 'incalculable value' (WSA T/A Swindon).

Bath and Bristol. Swindon would be the convenient point at which to change to and from more powerful engines to tackle the western section. Furthermore, some kind of premises would in any case be necessary at Swindon, both to accommodate banking and pilot engines, and as a station to serve the junction with the Cheltenham line. Centralizing repairs there as well would be a sensible economy.

Gooch noted also that a suitable, level site was available in the angle formed by the junction of the two lines, and that the canal existed nearby, which would enable coal at a reasonable price to be brought

Daniel Gooch was appointed to the GWR staff in 1837, and in September 1840 proposed to Brunel that the company's 'principal engine establishment' and a large station be built at Swindon. Three weeks later the board of directors agreed. He served as Superintendent of Locomotive Engines until 1864, and was then GWR chairman until he died in 1889.

to the depot. The principal drawback of Swindon, in Gooch's mind, was a poor water supply, but that in the last resort might be remedied by using the canal.

Soon after receiving the letter Gooch and Brunel visited the site, taking their lunch with them. The reality of the lunch is attested by Gooch's diary, and the story of the picnic, 'on the greensward which was then where the platform is now', was described in picturesque detail (including blossoming furze and frisking rabbits) by Richard Jefferies in an essay about Swindon published in 1875. Jefferies apparently was not aware of it when he wrote an earlier account of Swindon's origins in 1867, and in 1875 he wrongly attributes it to determining the line of the railway – this of course had been done much earlier, before Gooch worked for the Great Western. By 1913 the picnic legend ended with a stone, or even a sandwich, being thrown to decide upon the actual site of the railway works. Wittingly or unwittingly the foundation of plebeian New Swindon thereby paralleled that of its Wiltshire rival, patrician New Salisbury, whose site had been chosen (according to one version of the legend) by the flight of an arrow, shot by the bishop from the ramparts of Old Sarum Castle.

Whatever truth lies behind the primeval railway sandwich story, Brunel agreed with Gooch about his choice of Swindon, and the decision was endorsed by the Great Western Railway board of directors on 6 October 1840. But the apparently cogent operational reasons for the decision advanced by Gooch are by no means the whole story. Several recent authors have pointed out the impracticabilities of the scheme. In the first place the problem of water supply had not been adequately resolved. In fact poor water and sanitation were to blight the railway village and therefore the company's employees for many years. In the second place there was no obvious reason why the repair works should be cited alongside a depot for operational locomotives, especially on what was in effect a virgin site with no pool of skilled labour available. In the third place, while it was true that the canal at Swindon offered a cheap coal supply from areas not at the time accessible by railway, the same could be argued about Bristol, Bath or Chippenham, which were all much closer to the Somerset coalfield. Would not Bristol, where labour, water, housing and coal were all obtainable, have made better sense? Or Chippenham, then more populous than Swindon, which did indeed begin to develop as a railway manufacturing town?

To explain Gooch's preference for Swindon there have been suggestions that he was in some sense implicated in land deals, or was being offered a commission on profits by speculators; and it has been observed that by 1852 he was able to spend £13,400 (a considerable fortune at Victorian prices) on buying Nythe Farm near Wanborough. Clearly he could have had financial interests in developing Swindon which he never declared, and it would be naive to think that no private consultations ever took place between Gooch and prominent Swindonians. It would be particularly interesting, for example, to know whether any deals were done with the Wilts and Berks Canal, and its chairman, Ambrose Goddard, which were not revealed to the respective companies' directors.

But there is probably no need to tarnish the reputation of Daniel Gooch in order to explain his advocacy of Swindon. Britain between 1837 and 1842 was in severe recession, and this not only applied the brakes to new railway schemes, but also forced companies which were already committed to building lines to seek economies wherever possible. The Great Western was in particular difficulty since building costs had far outstripped estimates. Now the site at Swindon for the locomotive repair works recommended by Gooch already belonged to a railway company, the Cheltenham and Great Western Union. It is not known how or why the company acquired it, but it was a valuable asset, since transferring it to the Great Western enabled the smaller company to extract certain operating concessions from the larger, and the larger to acquire the site for its works with virtually no expenditure at all.

The next problem which the impoverished Great Western board had to face was the cost of building workers' housing, and an appropriate station complex for the railway junction. Gooch's plan offered the solution. He had made out a persuasive case for Swindon as the point at which engines should be changed. The resulting delay to the train could best be occupied and disguised by providing passengers with refreshments. Such a concept was of course perfectly familiar to travellers brought up on stagecoaches, and it was already practised at Wolverton (now part of Milton Keynes), the equivalent point on the London and Birmingham Railway, where railway works had just been completed – alongside a canal, to boot. By February 1841, four months after Gooch's recommendation had been approved, the company was ready

Brunel and Gooch are viewed as the Romulus and Remus of Swindon, but it is Brunel who has the higher profile. The statue of the town's 19th-century hero (a copy of that on the Victoria Embankment in London) gazes over the shopping centre that bears his name, to the tower called after Swindon's 20th-century hero, David Murray John.

to announce that it had made a deal whereby a construction firm would build the station and the railway village at its own expense, in return for the exclusive franchise of the refreshment facility, and the rents of the workers' cottages. By choosing Swindon, therefore, the company obtained its station, its workers' housing and the site of its works for nothing.

Gideon Mantell paid a last visit to Swindon in 1846. By then the station, the works and much of the railway village had been built. But 1846 was another important year in Swindon's evolution. The works, as we have seen, were designed for the repair of existing locomotives. In 1846, for the first time, new locomotives were manufactured at the works, and Swindon's revolution was fulfilled.

The first-class refreshment rooms at Swindon Junction station, engraved for a guide to the Great Western Railway by George Measom, published in 1852. The decor was a good deal more impressive than the food or the service.

4
A GOD OF STEAM

LIKE CREWE, Swindon during the 1840s rose from obscurity to become a household name. 'Swindon, all-important Swindon,' boasted a promotional guidebook to the Great Western Railway in 1852; 'who that knows aught of railways, or railway travelling, has not heard of Swindon's world-wide reputation, as well for the vastness of its workshops and engine depot, as for the admirable and splendid accommodation that it furnishes to the way-worn traveller?' A page of mouthwatering grandiloquence follows about the station refreshment rooms, ending with the opinion that, 'here we have a close approximation to perfection, accompanied, too, with undeviating civility, and a moderate tariff'.

The guidebook writer, replete no doubt with free helpings of the banbury-cakes and sherry-cobler which he eulogised, was spot on in his opinion that Swindon's reputation was made by its refreshment rooms. But it was not the reputation that Swindon might have wished. Despite the architecturally impressive surroundings, travellers did not share his enthusiasm, either about the quality or price of the 'choice refections'; indeed the nickname 'Swindleum' began to be applied to the establishment. Brunel himself was among the first to complain, within months of its opening. His letter to the caterer has often been quoted, in which he denies calling the coffee 'inferior' – he had actually called it 'bad roasted corn'. Older travellers perhaps recalled to mind the similar 'rip-off' mentality of innkeepers during the coaching era. Unfortunately for Swindon, it was the enforced refreshment stop and the exorbitant prices that travellers first encountered, which stuck in their memories

– these, rather than the other themes with which the present chapter is concerned: the locomotive works, the railway village, and the effect of the new town on the old. So we had better dispose of this embarrassing topic first.

Swindon Junction Station, with its elaborate refreshment rooms and hotel, was built in 1841-2 by J D and C Rigby, a London firm of builders, at their own expense, and its architecture survived largely unscathed until redevelopment of the site began in July 1972. The buildings comprised two two-story blocks with basements, linked by a footbridge which straddled the main line. The ornate refreshment rooms, for first and second class passengers (segregated) only, were at ground floor level, with kitchens below and hotel above.

As part of the deal Rigbys were leased the sole catering franchise at Swindon for 99 years on a peppercorn rent. In the early days a change of engine at Swindon was an operational necessity, as we have seen, and

Two early views of Swindon Junction station, from Measom's 1852 guide.

The surviving building of the original railway station, built by Rigbys in 1841-2 for the GWR.

so the company agreed that all trains would make a stop of about ten minutes at Swindon. This would be the only refreshment stop between London and Bristol. Rigbys sublet and eventually sold this franchise, but the ten-minute stop was rigorously enforced by the caterer long after the change of engine was no longer necessary. This exasperating delay, along with the exorbitant prices charged for mediocre food, continued to irritate the company and its passengers until 1895, when the GWR paid the princely sum of £100,000 to buy out the franchise-holder. By then, of course, the Swindon refreshment rooms, and by association the town itself, had become the butt of music-hall humour – the ignominy of much maligned Swindon had begun.

The locomotive depot and repair works, sanctioned by the board in October 1840, were begun in 1841 and completed before the end of

Edward Snell's water-colour bird's-eye-view of Swindon works to the left, railway station and t

1842, for regular use from January 1843. Brunel was responsible for designing them to Gooch's requirements (the job was probably delegated to an assistant, T.H. Bertram), and Rigbys were employed as contractors. At the heart of the original works were two large sheds, abutting to form a T-shape. The cross-piece of the T, parallel with the Bristol line

in the centre, and railway village with St Mark's church to the right. It was painted in 1849.

to its south, was the engine shed; adjoining it on its northern side was the repair shop. Other necessary buildings, including the smiths' shops, wagon shops, the erecting shop and the offices, were arranged around this T, rather like quadrangles around an Oxford college. Some elements of this original design, though much modified, have survived,

The engine house in 1846, where routine maintenance to locomotives was carried out. It could accommodate 36 engines, like horses in stables.

notably part of the English Heritage building, one wall of STEAM, and Churchward House. The master of the establishment, under Daniel Gooch, was a Scotsman, Archibald Sturrock. Like Gooch he was in his early twenties, and the two men had become friends before either joined the GWR. He stayed with the company, as works superintendent, until 1850, then was employed for sixteen years by the Great Northern Railway. In 1866, aged 50, he retired, but did not die until New Year's Day, 1909, 42 years later.

The works quickly progressed from repairing to manufacturing rolling stock, including carriages and wagons, and (a revolutionary step for an operating company in those days) in February 1846 the first locomotive, named *Premier*, was produced. The GWR, locked in controversy over the merits of the broad gauge compared with its rivals' narrow (now standard) gauge, was eager to show its superiority, and in January 1846 Gooch was instructed to build, 'a colossal locomotive working with all speed'. A mere thirteen weeks later the engine, *Great Western*, was running, and showed that it was capable of hauling passenger trains over long distances at an average speed of nearly 60 mph. Twenty-eight more express passenger locomotives were built at Swindon between 1846 and 1851, as well as many smaller goods engines. They established the works at the forefront of railway technology, and its reputation was underscored in 1851 when one of its progeny, *Lord of the Isles*, was exhibited at the Great Exhibition.

This western façade of STEAM Museum incorporates the smiths' shop in the foreground, and the machine and fitting shop beyond, both of 1846. The smiths' shop was later heightened, but some of its original masonry remains.

But reputation was not enough. Swindon began its manufacturing career during the railway mania of 1844-7, when companies such as the GWR over-reached themselves with ambitious plans for expansion. Following the repeal of the Corn Laws in 1846 and the influx of cheap imported grain the stock market collapsed in 1847. The GWR was in serious financial trouble and retrenched its operations. At Swindon the workforce had risen from about 400 in 1843 to 1,800 by 1847,

A promotional photograph (from the very early days of the medium) of Lord of the Isles, positioned in front of St Mark's Church. The locomotive, an early product of the works, was displayed at the Great Exhibition of 1851.

after which it was savagely cut to 600. Several senior officers, including Sturrock, resigned rather than face a cut in salary. Recovery was gradual, but at Swindon it was helped by a new dimension during the 1850s, as the GWR acquired Midland companies operating narrow (standard) gauge lines, and required locomotives and rolling stock for them.

Railway engineering in general, and Swindon works in particular, was the high technology of the 1840s. It demanded a workforce quite different from either the uncouth navvies who built the lines, or the pastoral farmhands who inhabited the neighbouring north Wiltshire countryside. Skilled engineers and fabricators, like oilfield workers in the North Sea during the 1980s, computer programmers during the 1990s, and website designers in the 2020s commanded a high premium, and travelled to Swindon from all over the country to work hard for high wages. Analysis of the 1851 census for New Swindon shows that nearly 15% of the population originated in Scotland or Northern England, and nearly 10% in London and the South-East; the equivalent proportions in Old Swindon were 1% and 4%. A study of the careers of many New Swindon pioneers has shown that some were 'headhunted' by Gooch and Sturrock from places where they had worked previously – Dundee, the North-East and south Lancashire. There seems even to have been a kind of recruitment agency operating for Gooch in Liverpool.

It was clear to the GWR board when they decided to site the works at Swindon that accommodation for their employees would have to be provided. We have already described the deal whereby Rigbys built at their own expense cottages for the workforce on land which the GWR had purchased, in return for fixed rents from the occupants. It is time now to examine the outcome of this arrangement.

The development of New Swindon as a community may be compared with two other English towns which owed their origins to railway works on 'green field' sites, Crewe in Cheshire, and Wolverton in Buckinghamshire, now part of Milton Keynes. Wolverton's railway works were begun by the London and Birmingham Railway in 1838 and, like Swindon's, were sited at the point on the line where a change of engine was necessary and a canal was at hand. The population grew from 417 in 1831 to 2,070 in 1851, and the new town was built as a grid of 242 redbrick terraced houses, with a church, a school and several pubs. That Wolverton was in the GWR directors' minds when they sanctioned the development at Swindon is clear from their report, in which the place is specifically mentioned. Crewe, the creation of the Grand Junction Railway, was exactly contemporary with Swindon, since its railway works were begun in 1841. Early housing, some with Gothic detailing, included a range of accommodation reflecting the status of its occupants within the works.

At Swindon two blocks of four parallel streets were laid out and built up with terraces of cottages, largely between 1842 and 1846. The streets took their names from destinations of the trains which passed nearby – Bristol, Bath, Exeter and Taunton comprised the western block, London, Oxford, Reading and Faringdon the eastern block. The western block was built up quickly, mostly in 1842 and 1843, with the eastern block following during 1845-7, though a few were built later, in 1853-4. The terraces are of two-storey cottages, generally with one or two bedrooms, and built of local Swindon stone with some dressings (quoining and around windows and doors) of Oolitic limestone, possibly won during the building of the cuttings leading into Box Tunnel. Between the two blocks of terraces, running north towards the works entrance, was a wide boulevard-like area originally called High Street, and by 1848 larger houses and shops had been erected facing it at the end of each terrace. The Mechanics' Institute and Medical Fund Hospital were subsequently built on this open area, and it was renamed Emlyn Square after Viscount Emlyn, a GWR chairman. Most of the railway

Although superficially similar, because all are built of the local Swindon stone, with quoining and window and door surrounds of Bath stone, there are many variations in design, size and layout of the 300 cottages built between 1841 and 1847 within a grid of eight streets laid out in two blocks of four.

Because the cottages in the railway village were laid out to different specifications and sizes over a six-year period, but the street plan remained symmetrical, there were variations too in the alleys that gave them rear access. Rudimentary drainage running under the alleys from privies in the back yards was a source of squalor and ill-health in the early years.

village, as this estate is known, was purchased by the local authority in 1966, and renovated between 1969 and 1980. One cottage (which is, however, not typical of the estate as a whole, since it is later and larger than most) was opened as a museum in 1980, and was furnished and decorated to appear as it might have done in about 1900. It is currently (2023) maintained by the Mechanics Institution Trust and open occasionally to the public.

Since 1945, and perhaps before, a tradition has grown up in Swindon that the railway village was designed by the eminent Victorian architect and architectural writer, Sir Matthew Digby Wyatt. It is true that between 1852 and 1854 he collaborated with Brunel on the design of Paddington Station, and so had a connection with the GWR. But that was later. In 1841, when work began on the railway village, he was barely twenty, and was saving to go on the Grand Tour by working in a drawing office, and also undertaking small architectural commissions – a school in Wales, two houses near Dublin and a London factory building. While it is possible that Rigby's sought his help for Swindon, no connection with the project is mentioned by his biographers or appears in his list of works. Another objection to the theory of his involvement is that, although the railway village has a unified appearance, there are significant differences of architectural detail between the terraces, as if modifications were made as the building work progressed. Wyatt spent two years, 1844-6, touring on the continent, and so could not have been directly involved with the project as it took shape.

The railway village repays study nevertheless. The problem of housing large working communities close to new industrial complexes

The kitchen of 34 Faringdon Road, preserved as it might have been in 1900, although probably little different from when built in 1847.

was not new in the 1840s. It had been faced by colliery and mill owners in the Midlands and North for several decades, as the industrial revolution invaded remote and unpopulated areas. Some of the resulting employer housing was of very poor quality, but by the 1830s two arguments had emerged for providing reasonably good living conditions for the workforce – that they helped to recruit suitable and desirable employees, and that they enhanced productivity by reducing illness and improving morale. What had not yet emerged by 1840 were the conclusions of inquiries linking poor sanitation and water supply with disease, which led to the passing of public health legislation in 1848. Nor was the era of philanthropic housing schemes, initiated by benevolent societies and conscientious employers, yet under way – although it was just beginning, and a few notable experiments had been tried.

It was against this background that the railway village emerged. Despite the aura of paternalism which the company later managed to

At the ends of each street were larger and grander houses and shops, several of which became pubs. They were not part of the housing contract with Rigby's, and were built by another contractor to designs by Brunel. They faced on to what was then a wide boulevard known as High Street, on which the Mechanics Institute and other community buildings were later erected.

convey, the GWR in the 1840s was not, and could not afford to be, a philanthropic organization. It could not justify to its shareholders what might be seen as unnecessary expenditure on moral or religious grounds. In fact it rather side-stepped responsibility for housing its workers through its deal with Rigby's. And Rigby's, driven no doubt by normal commercial considerations of the rate of return on their investment, built to a standard which they considered would warrant the rent which skilled engineering workers could be expected to pay. If that standard was quite high, it was because Rigby's had saved money by not having had to purchase the site, there was a bountiful supply of good building stone, and the intended occupants were comparatively well paid. The main drawback, which was exacerbated by early overcrowding in the village, was the old bugbear which Gooch had identified in his original report, the problem of water supply and drainage.

Edward Snell, who became Assistant Works Manager in about 1849, and who painted the famous panorama of New Swindon in that year, was one of the first inhabitants of the railway village, arriving at the end of February 1843. Soon afterwards he wrote in his diary:

> For my part I hate it and haven't been well since I've been here . . . A precious place it is at present, not a knocker or a scraper in the whole place. Most of the houses very damp and containing only two rooms . . . Not a drop of water to be had but what comes from the tenders or out of ditches and what little we do get is as thick as mud – not fit for a jackass to drink. The Company make the men pay most extortionate rents for these bits of huts, too – 3s. 6d. for a single and 7s. for a double cottage and won't allow any of the men in their employ to sell anything whatever. We have a couple of Doctors' Shops which are pretty frequently visited, a Great Western Sick Club, a school . . . and a chapel.

Snell's experience confirms the impression of squalid, overcrowded and unhealthy conditions given by other sources. Smallpox, typhus and cholera occurred there during the first decade. Admittedly living standards may have seemed worse to Snell – he was born in Barnstaple and apprenticed in Bath – than to other newcomers accustomed to urban overcrowding in Sunderland or Liverpool. His mention of the various social amenities already available in New Swindon is remarkable,

A GOD OF STEAM

because, written in 1843, it antedates the usually accepted date for any of them. He cannot have made them up, however, and the existence of the chapel is confirmed by a document preserved at Gloucester. This records that in June 1843 a group of Methodists were holding services in a room next to the Golden Lion Inn near the Swindon Railroad Station; they were under the leadership of a Wesleyan minister from Marlborough with a wonderfully Old Testament name, Zephaniah Job.

During the 1840s and 1850s the amenities mentioned by Snell, and several others, became established in their own buildings. They were supported by the company in various ways, and some acquired GWR as a handle to their names, but in general they did not originate with the company and were not officially funded. Thus the GWR church (St Mark's) and the GWR School next to it resulted from a bequest in 1842 by C.H. Gibbs, a director, and were built on land donated by

St Mark's Church, of 1843-5, is contemporary with the village, its tall spire and generous dimensions very visible from the railway tracks, presumably to emphasise to GWR customers that the company was concerned with its employees' spiritual and moral welfare. The GWR did not in fact build it, though it was the result of a bequest by one of its directors.

Colonel Vilett. St Mark's Church, 'all spikes and prickles outside', was completed in 1845 on land immediately west of the railway village. In an essay published in 1952 Sir John Betjeman paid the church, and the community which worshipped there, a unique compliment: 'One cannot call it a convenient site . . . But it is a strong church and though it is not much to look at, it is for me the most loved church in England.' The

The provision of public parks for recreation was advocated in a government report of 1833, largely to ameliorate living conditions in already squalid industrial suburbs. As a result municipal parks began to appear from about 1840. The GWR Park, donated to (not purchased by) the company by a local landowner, dates from 1844 and so is a very early and unusual example, providing an amenity for a town still in its infancy, with open land all around.

school opened during the same year, and was soon suffering the same overcrowding as the rest of the village. In 1847 it had 168 pupils and only two teachers. The GWR park, abutting the school and church, was given by Colonel Vilett to the company as a public amenity in 1844.

The two most prestigious organizations stemming from the early years of the railway village were the mechanics' institute and the medical fund. Gooch claimed to have started the institute in January

1844, in response to complaints from the neighbouring gentry about drunkenness and disorder: 'I got together those of the workmen whose moral character was superior to their fellows and formed them into a Workmen's Institute.' In fact its genesis probably lay in an informal lending library begun by employees a few months' earlier. Under the name 'New Swindon Mechanics' Institution' the organization rapidly grew, and provided not only evening classes and the library, but also entertainments of various kinds, including theatre, concerts and dances. One event organised by the institute in 1849, a free excursion to Oxford, proved so successful that an annual 'Trip' by train developed as a kind of works' outing, and ultimately as the annual holiday for employees and their families. In 1855 the mechanics' institute moved into purpose-built premises in the centre of the railway village, which had been built by a company set up for the purpose and chaired by the works superintendent. An octagonal market hall adjoined the institute building. The mechanics' institute library continued to function as a public library for Swindon until the second world war.

The GWR Mechanics Institute (or more properly Institution) was established within the works in 1844 and the present sadly dilapidated building was erected in 1854. It contained meeting rooms, a theatre and a library and reading rooms, and had an octagonal market attached to its southern end. After the closure of the works in 1986 it became neglected, although a vigorous campaign to restore it has been active for many years.

The octagonal open market hall attached to the southern side of the institute. After it was demolished in 1891 the institute building was extended. The main entrance (in 2023, below) was boarded up and overgrown.

The GWR Medical Fund Society traced its origins to the period of distress caused by the lay-offs and short-time working introduced in 1847. It appears to have been an employee-led initiative to create a fund which would pay the surgeon to attend both working and laid-off staff and their families. To pay for the scheme every employed man would pay a small weekly subscription; but Gooch successfully sought company blessing, and assistance in the form of a rent-free house in the railway village for the surgeon, and an annual stipend for the surgeon to cover attendance to accidents at work. A society was formed to administer the fund, and this eventually grew to such proportions that in 1871 it built and administered its own hospital next to the Mechanics' Institute, and then in 1892 swimming baths and a dispensary across Faringdon Road. Decades later the society was one of the models studied when the National Health Service was established.

The GWR Medical Fund Society stemmed from the health concerns of the employees, who paid their subscriptions into it. It had the company's blessing and support, and became so important that in 1871 it built its own hospital.

The swimming baths and dispensary were the last large community building associated with the GWR, opened in 1892. The blue plaque commemorates the medical fund society's role as a model for the founding of the National Health Service.

One other prominent establishment of the period was intended to solve the overcrowding problem. This was a lodging-house for single men, which Richard Jefferies claimed could accommodate 500, and was 'a vast place, with innumerable rooms and corridors'. It was begun in 1849 and completed in 1852, but the austere pile was immediately unpopular, and was nicknamed the 'Barracks'. Little occupied, it was later turned into flats for an influx of Welsh workers, then sold to become a

This somewhat overpowering building has had various careers. It was built and opened in 1855 as a hostel or barracks to accommodate single men employed in the works. Never popular, it became a Methodist chapel in 1867, and then from 1962 housed the railway museum. When that moved to STEAM in a former works building in 2000 it became a performance space, and is now called The Platform.

chapel, and from 1962 until replaced by STEAM in 2000 was employed to house the railway museum. It is now 'The Platform', a performance venue.

In 1850, and for many years to follow, there was open countryside stretching down the hillside which separated old, respectable Swindon from this alien aberration of the railway revolution. How strange, how disconcerting, how fascinating it all must have seemed to the Wiltshire countryman – the unintelligible accents of the newcomers, the fearsome power unleashed by the engines, the massive buildings, spanking new. That intervening mile of grass and agriculture was doubtless a comfort to many in Old Swindon, but it was not far enough to allow the town to vegetate in some xenophobic cocoon. In fact the effect on it of New Swindon was profound. A government inspector, called in to examine the town's public health, reported in 1850 that: 'The old town of Swindon has materially increased in numbers and wealth since the completion of the railway. The houses built have been of a superior class; and the tenants, being more or less connected with the railway, are a well-behaved and intelligent class of persons.'

So this was one consequence of the railway works, that some of the better-paid employees found their way up the hill and made their homes in Old Swindon. But many more of the newcomers, wives and young children especially, were familiar with the trek across the fields for another reason. In the early years of the railway village there were few shops, and most food and provisions consumed in New Swindon had to be purchased in the old town, and carried back down Eastcott Hill or Prospect, which were then narrow field paths. 'Those were rosy days for Old Swindon shopkeepers and publicans', recalled an old man who had grown up at Prospect in the 1860s. The railway workers were paid fortnightly, on alternate Fridays, and then large sums of money changed hands in Old Town.

Victoria Street, as it was known in the 1840s (now Victoria Road) was built up with houses and shops of architectural pretension with Italianate and Venetian styling, pandering to early Victorian taste. The house on the left displays a plaque to local author Richard Jefferies, who lived here briefly in the 1860s.

Like many towns at this period, Old Swindon aspired to a market hall, and growing administrative responsibilities needed a Town Hall. The five-bay classical structure with central pediment, and open on the ground floor when built in 1853, combined these functions, and was joined in 1866 by a corn exchange, with an elaborate tower over its entrance. The complex was never a great success, and had a multitude of careers, including wine merchant (whose letterhead, above, proclaims Victorian grandeur), skating rink, cinema, ballroom (the Locarno, and fondly remembered) and bingo hall. Since the 1970s it has sunk into a long, though not quite terminal, decline, as seen in 2023 (below).

A symbol of Old Swindon's prosperity after the railway town arrived below the hill is the former Wilts and Dorset Bank, one of several banks nearby, built on the corner of Wood Street in 1884. It provides a striking contrast to the earlier and more modest country-town shops in High Street.

There is no doubt that wealth created in the railway works stimulated Old Swindon's economy. But even without that the town seems to have been doing well during the 1840s. A directory description published in 1848 was particularly up-beat about (Old) Swindon's progress. New streets were being laid out, the general appearance of the town was improving, and the shops now equalled those of Bath and Cheltenham. A large assembly room had recently been added to the Goddard Arms, and there were plans to build a Town Hall and market house. The old church was too small for the growing population, and so there were proposals to replace it with a new one. The cattle market was making a great name for itself, and the flourishing quarries were major employers. All in all, 'Swindon may now, perhaps, be said to be one of the most flourishing and promising towns in Wiltshire'.

The permanent (as opposed to transient) population of Old Swindon in 1841 cannot be accurately deduced from the census, but was probably of the order of 1,800–1,850. In 1851 it was 2,294, which represented a rise of about 25%. To accommodate the extra families new houses were built and new streets laid out. They were given patriotic names – Britannia Place, Victoria Street, Albert Street, Union Row – and most of them have survived to the present day. But for all its pretensions the expanding town had problems. Sanitation was poor, water sources were becoming polluted, and disease was rife. The inspector called in to report in 1850 discovered that life expectancy had reduced from over 36 years in the whole parish during the 1820s to 29 years in Old Town in the 1840s. He recommended that a sewerage and water supply system be provided for the town, and that a local board be set up to oversee it.

However different Old and New Swindon might have appeared, they could not for long escape the fundamental problem common to them both – that the provision of infrastructure services was not keeping pace with the rising population. These and other growing pains were to continue for another fifty years, until Old and New disappeared, and Swindon became simply Swindon again.

The landmark broach spire of Old Town's replacement parish church, Christ Church, designed by Sir George Gilbert Scott and completed in 1851.

5
BRICK-BUILT BREEDING BOXES

THE NEXT CLUE to decoding Swindon involves statistics. Swindon in 1851 had a population of 4,879, almost equally divided between the old and new towns. A half-century later, in 1901, the census returned a total of 45,006, and no longer distinguished between old and new. This was because in the previous year the two communities had united to become a municipal borough. During the same half-century the population of England and Wales rose by 81%; but that of Wiltshire rose by only 8%, and if Swindon is left out of the reckoning, the rest of Wiltshire's population actually declined by 8%. Swindon meanwhile increased by nothing short of 822%. The goal of the present chapter is to account for this astounding jump (far greater than anything achieved since 1901), and to examine its impact on the Swindon which we see around us.

We left the railway works in trouble at the end of the 1840s, with its workforce slashed to 600. By 1900 the payroll had risen by leaps and bounds to about 11,500. Four interrelated factors were responsible not only for the leaps and bounds, but also for intervening episodes of setback and disappointment. First were periods of expansion and retrenchment in the national economy of Victorian England. Second were technical improvements and new legislation affecting railways. Third were the fortunes of the Great Western Railway, as it built new lines and took over competitors, but also teetered towards bankruptcy. And fourth were decisions taken by the company's directors to centralise its engineering activities at Swindon.

Recovery after the desperate days of 1847-9 was accomplished at first by diversifying to build components for bridges and other civil engineering works. Later, in 1854, the GWR purchased rival companies in the Midlands which used the narrow, or standard, gauge. This resulted in the need for new locomotives and rolling stock, which Swindon began to produce in 1855. Then in 1860-1 Daniel Gooch persuaded his board to build a rolling mill at the works, which would produce better and cheaper iron rails than they could obtain from outside contractors, and would also be a way of recycling scrap iron from Swindon's other manufacturing processes. During another railway boom in the 1860s the GWR, saddled with its broad gauge, was beleaguered by competing railways. They tried to encroach on its territory with plans for standard gauge lines, and large sums were spent on legal actions opposing them, as well as in proposing new lines of its own. In 1866 the company had overreached itself and was almost bankrupt; it was only through skilful negotiation with its creditors that Daniel Gooch, newly appointed chairman, drew the GWR back from the abyss.

The forbidding south wall of the carriage works, built 1869-71 between the railway village and the mainline tracks.

BRICK-BUILT BREEDING BOXES

This cloud of financial ruin had a silver lining for Swindon. The company had since 1865 been thinking about establishing new carriage works at Oxford. Gooch now persuaded his board that Swindon would be a cheaper alternative, because company-owned land was already available, in the area between the railway village and the main Bristol line. Here, abutting Bristol Street and London Street, the carriage works were begun in 1868, and it is their fortress-like façade of stone and glass, some 350m long, which for over a century separated living Swindon from working Swindon. A decade of expansion and prosperity for Swindon works followed, stimulated largely by the gradual changeover from broad to standard gauge. Orders for new locomotives and rolling stock to meet the change kept Swindon busy, and justified wholesale modernization of the factory.

As the works continued to grow, by the end of the century the first buildings were erected west of Rodbourne Road. The pattern store was built in 1897 to house the precious wooden patterns from which castings were made. Heavily fireproofed, the building was further protected by massive water tanks on the roof.

The boom ended in 1877/8, and no further expansion took place at the works until 1887. Nationally these were years of severe depression, and one consequence was a reduction in demand for rail traffic. The GWR found itself over-resourced, and imposed a freeze on orders for new stock. Swindon suffered less than some other establishments, however, as the company chose to centralise work on its largest plant, and by judicious accounting, routine repairs, and work on new safety modifications, the railway works managed to tick over. This difficult period came to a sudden end in 1887, with new orders, the implementation of new safety requirements, and the run-up to the

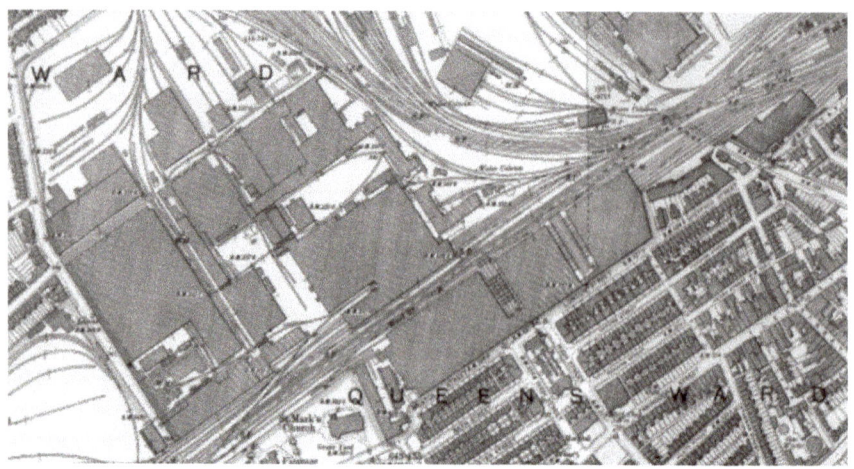

The railway works, mapped in 1899. The Bristol line runs diagonally from top right (the junction station) to bottom left, where it crosses Rodbourne Road; the rectangular building west of the road is the newly erected pattern store. The carriage works lies south of the railway line with the railway village beyond. The North Wilts Canal was still a feature; it enters the map halfway down the right edge and runs beneath the tracks.

final conversion from broad to standard gauge in 1892. As the national recession drew to a close in the mid-1890s the GWR was poised to set new standards of comfort and sophistication, with improved locomotive and carriage design, and an assured future for Swindon at the head of railway technology.

Clearly, in charting the progress of the railway works to the dawn of the new century, when it employed over 11,500 (most of them male breadwinners), we have accounted for much of Swindon's spectacular rise in population. A few years later, in 1908, it was estimated that nearly 80% of Swindon's male workforce were employed by the GWR. So many men inside the works left a pool of employable wives and daughters outside, and this attracted clothing factories to Swindon. The largest, Compton's in Sheppard Street, had 1,000 employees in the 1890s, and very appropriately its work included the manufacture of GWR uniforms. Even so, relatively few Swindon women (7.2% in 1908) were in paid employment.

What about the men who did not work 'inside' (as employment in the railway works was always referred to), or elsewhere on the railway system? Some at Old Town were quarrymen, or were connected with the agriculture of the surrounding area. Many more worked in the various retail and service industries which the growing town required. A particular need, of course, was for houses to accommodate the multitude of newcomers, and an army of building workers moved in. They were the true creators of Victorian Swindon, and much of their legacy remains to the present day.

Sir John Betjeman was commissioned to write a study of architecture in Swindon to commemorate the combined borough's half-century in 1950. From the beautifully polished essay which resulted we may gather that he found the town interesting, but unattractive. He drew a clear distinction between architecture, of which he discovered few examples and little to admire, and building, of which he found a great deal, and much to criticise. But in his 1950 work he could not be too rude about his paymasters' town. In another essay published in 1952 he was more blunt: 'For there is no doubt that Swindon *is* superficially ugly. That pretty model village of the eighteen-forties has developed a red brick rash which stretches up the hill to Old Swindon and strangles it.'

The red brick rash climbing Eastcott Hill, the old route to the hilltop town.

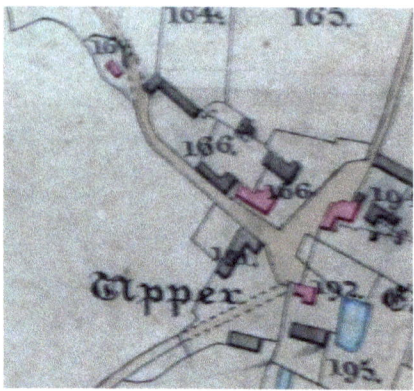
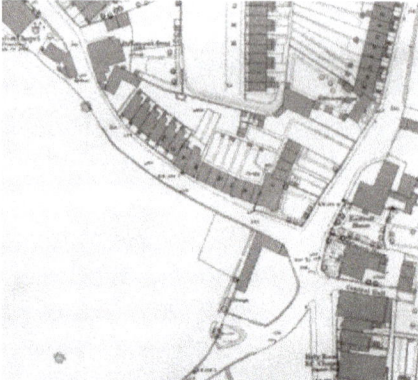

Upper Eastcott Farm in 1840 (top left), as depicted on the tithe map, and in 1886 (top right) after York Place and other terraces had been built by speculators. F H Spencer (right) was brought up in York Place. Swindon Town Hall was built shortly afterwards in the D-shaped plot to the south and Regent Circus was formed.

The 'red brick rash' is entirely the result of piecemeal and usually small-scale development by builders and speculators, who responded to the housing demands of the new population, and who, in the absence of any local government planning policy, were constrained only by market forces and the availability of land. A good example of this process at work is described in the autobiography of an influential educationalist, F H Spencer, who was born in 1870 in a house (no longer standing) adjoining what is now Regent Circus. Spencer recalls a character whom he called 'Old Charlie', a tallish, thin Yorkshireman, who had made money as a skilled mechanic at the works, and who had invested it during the 1850s in buying Upper Eastcott farmhouse and six small stone cottages that went with it. On to these he built a terrace of six brick houses and a small shop, which he let out to tenants. Spencer's parents lived in one of these houses for about thirty years, and he remembered as a teenager helping Old Charlie to work out the charges necessary to make a minimum of 7.5% on a gross outlay in cottage property.

Charlie the Yorkshireman, who was 'no worse than the others' according to Spencer, called his terrace 'York Place'. Other speculators attained a kind of immortality for themselves and their families by

BRICK-BUILT BREEDING BOXES

enshrining them in street names. John Henry Harding Sheppard was a brewer in Old Town who owned land near the railway station and at Kingshill. Four streets in the Queenstown area between the railway village and the station divided up his name between them during the 1870s, and after his death his son, who retired to Kent, built up a field at Kingshill as Ashford, Folkestone, Hythe, Kent and Maidstone Roads. George Whitehead, as well as property speculator and builder, had careers as a shopkeeper, musician and publican. His wife Beatrice, his daughter Florence, and the composer after whom his shop was named, Handel, all have adjoining streets to themselves in Gorse Hill, but his own street, Whitehead Street, lies on the other side of the tracks, at least a ten-minute walk away – which, it has to be said, is a novel way of hinting at domestic disharmony.

Examples such as these could be multiplied from all over Victorian and Edwardian Swindon. For instance, the partners of an Old Town firm of solicitors, Messrs Butterworth, Rose, and Morrison, each have a street for their surnames, and George Montagu Butterworth and Sydney Bruce Morrison have both immortalised their middle names as well. More curiously, Edmund Jones built Maxwell Street, and James Maxwell built Edmund Street. Many other road names took their cue from the patriotic fervour of the later nineteenth century, or from national or GWR dignitaries. A few stem from allegiance to the builder's native place. Maxwell's firm came from Manchester (hence Manchester Road), Linslade Street was named by a native of the Bedfordshire town, Cheltenham and Gloucester Streets derive from the building society responsible, and there were two small neighbourhoods with Oxford overtones – Carfax, Merton, Oriel and Turl Streets; and Cobden, Harcourt and Iffley Roads – which were both the work of the Oxford Building Society and its successors.

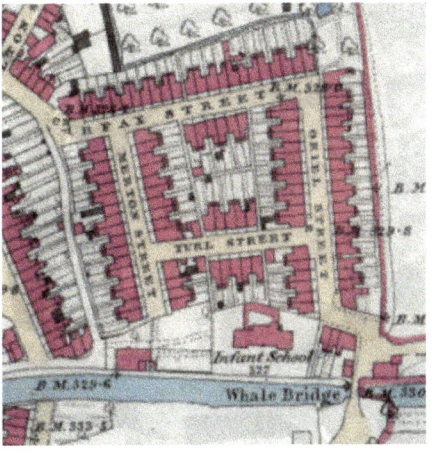

A square of terraced houses built by the Oxford Building Society, and so named after Oxford streets. Whale Bridge across the canal is explained overleaf.

'The people who planned these streets,' mused J B Priestley in disdain, as he explored Swindon on a dreary evening fifty years later, 'must have been thinking and dreaming hard about the next world, not this one: it is the only charitable conclusion.' But the reality was that they did very little planning at all, the majority of them lived elsewhere, and, like Old Charlie, they were thinking and dreaming mainly about their 7.5% return. They bid for individual plots of land or whole fields as they came on to the market, and either developed them immediately, if the works were booming and houses were in demand, or let them lie fallow for a few years, if economic conditions were less good. From sale catalogues, maps, directories and building byelaw records it is possible to trace their activities in great detail, but for present purposes a summary will suffice.

During the 1840s the railway village was the main area of growth, but speculative housing was already beginning to appear in the area of Westcott Place, following the line of a much older track known as the 'Fleet' or 'Fleetway'. And because railway works construction stimulated a temporary burst of activity at the canal wharf, a beerhouse and terrace of houses was built nearby. The beerhouse took its name, 'The Whale,' from the shape of the canal bridge next to it, and the houses, 'Cetus

This mural, by Ken White, is painted on the end wall of a terrace of houses beside the canal, originally called Cetus Buildings after the Latin word for 'whale', Whale Bridge (see map on previous page) was so-called because of its shape. The mural in fact depicts Golden Lion Bridge, and the figures include Alfred Williams, who we shall encounter in chapter 6, with his wife, in the foreground, and Isambard Brunel lurking at the back.

Buildings', took their rather pretentious name from the beerhouse (*cetus* is Latin for a whale). A second place of refreshment, the Golden Lion Inn, was in business by 1843, and this became a pivotal landmark in the development of the town's street plan. It stood beside the canal next to a swing-bridge, the Golden Lion Bridge, and from this a track led southeast across the field to Upper Eastcott Farm, and thence up Eastcott Hill to Old Swindon.

Survivors (just) of the many cottages made into shops that once lined the main streets of Victorian New Swindon. These are in Fleet Street.

This bridge and track fixed the line of what was to become the next focus of private housing. During the 1850s terraces of small houses sprang up beside the track, which was then known along its whole length as Bridge Street. It was only later, during the 1860s and 1870s, that many of these houses were converted into shops, and then for the stretch of road south of Golden Lion Bridge a more stylish (even pretentious) name, Regent Street, was coined, perhaps as a joke at first, to reflect its new commercial status. The principal crossroad of the modern pedestrianised shopping centre now marks the site of the Golden Lion, but a few of the 1850s workers' houses still peep from behind and above shopfronts towards the northern end of Bridge Street and in Fleet Street.

Until the mid-1860s most of New Swindon, Regent Street apart, lay to the north of the Wilts and Berks Canal. Gooch's decision to build a rolling mill for iron rails at the works in 1861 attracted workers from the ironworks of South Wales. Initially they were housed with their families in the Barracks, but by 1864 a 'Welsh Colony' had been built for them between the railway village and Westcott Place. This was called Cambria Place, and had its own Welsh-speaking Baptist chapel. Further east, between the railway village and the angle formed by the junction of the North Wilts Canal with the Wilts and Berks, Mr Sheppard's field was built-up with the four roads of his name, John, Henry, Harding and Sheppard Streets.

Cambria Baptist Chapel, built for Welsh speakers recruited during the 1860s to make iron rails at the works.

It was a busy time for the railway works, as we have seen, with the new carriage works opening in 1868 and a full order book for locomotives continuing through much of the 1870s. These prosperous years, from about 1865 to 1877, found the property speculators and small-time builders busy too. Now a tide of red brick was about to begin creeping up the hill towards Old Swindon. Havelock Street and its neighbours now beneath the Brunel Centre were followed by the advance guard of terraces running south from what would later become Regent Circus and the Town Hall. Infilling occurred in the area between the railway village and the canal, now occupied by Farnsby Street and the Murray John building. And forays were made eastward across the North Wilts Canal towards the station. But large areas of farmland around Swindon were out of bounds to developers until 1885, because of a legal dispute over the inheritance of what remained of one of Swindon's former manors, the Vilett estate. This restriction led, not only to overcrowding on cramped sites which were available, but also to sporadic housebuilding in far-flung places, such as on the slopes of Kingshill, and north of the railway at Even Swindon and Gorse Hill.

At the works the wheels of progress ground to a halt in about 1877, as we have seen, and the influx of new population was stemmed. The housebuilding market did not revive until after 1885, by when the restriction on Vilett lands had been lifted. This enforced lull, whatever its economic consequences at the time, offered a pause for reflection. New Swindon, from being a chaotic jumble of uncontrolled accretions for the accommodation of railway workers, was developing into an important town, with its own commercial and retail areas, a form of local government (New Swindon Board of Health), and a variety of social and welfare activities provided by, or connected with, the main employer.

A plan of New Swindon showing lands belonging to the Vilett estate, outlined in red, which could not be developed until after 1885, together with the first proposals to build on them once they became available, centred on Commercial Road (WSA).

One consequence of this was that, when building recommenced after 1885, schemes were on a larger and grander scale. Three developments set out to alter the balance of Swindon. The first lay to the west of Regent Street and was centred on a new alignment, Commercial Road. The aim of the builders was to capture from Regent Street its trading supremacy. A market was built at its western end, where it met

Commercial Road (above), a new development of the 1890s, was made possible once the Vilett estate could be built over. In providing part of a link between Old Town and the railway village it adopted a completely different alignment from the older Regent Street, graphically illustrated by the map (opposite page, below). The older section of Havelock Street, aligned on Regent Street, thus made an abrupt change of direction halfway along to take its place as part of the new alignment. This newer section of Havelock Street, its terraced houses adapted as shops, and here seen from the Commercial Road end (below), now turns at its far end where it meets the Brunel Plaza, successor to the Victorian streets of terraced houses which once filled this area, as seen in the top half of the lower map opposite.

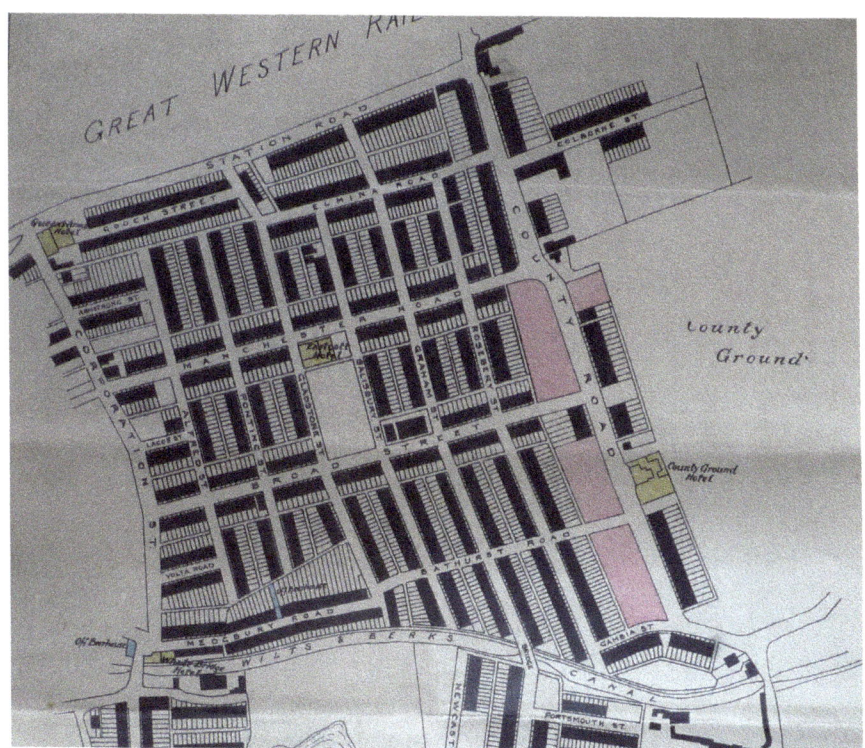

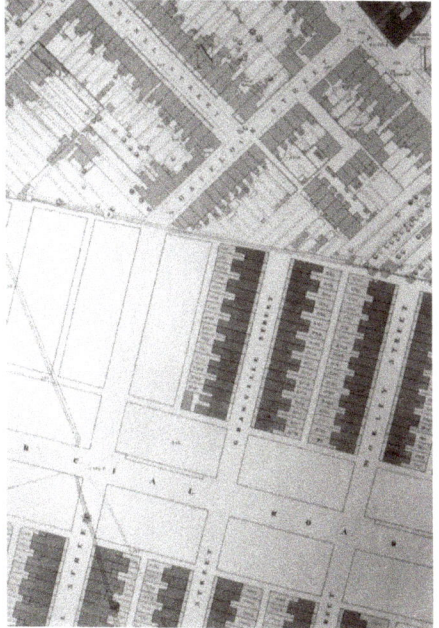

Whereas the lower map shows the Commercial Road development while it was taking place, the upper map, an estate plan, shows another area of the former Vilett estate, south-east of the railway station, entirely built up with terraced housing. This is the Manchester Road and Broad Street area, developed around 1900, and including streets named after prominent Victorian politicians (WSA).

the canal, and at the eastern end Regent Circus was laid out by 1889, around a blatantly municipal building, the Town Hall of 1891. The second scheme involved forging a proper link with the old town by creating a thoroughfare up

The offices of the New Swindon Local Board, when it was built in 1891, and destined to become the Town Hall of the combined Old and New Swindon in 1900. Also in 1900 York Square, the open area laid out in front of it, was renamed Regent Circus.

the hill. Victoria Road, as it was christened, was made up in 1888, and by 1900 houses and side streets had been built along much of its length. The third large-scale development, which took place during the years around 1900, filled with houses the area between the station and the canal, aligned on Manchester Road and Broad Street.

Alongside these giant modifications to the Swindon landscape the small opportunist builder continued his work of infilling odd plots and poking out into the suburbs. Furthermore – and this is often overlooked – Old Swindon too was growing, especially on its northern and western

BRICK-BUILT BREEDING BOXES

Eastcott Hill, New Swindon on its way up the hill (left)
Prospect Hill, Old Swindon on its way down (right).

edges. Here, according to Betjeman, we shall encounter the Victorian middle classes: 'Outcast from the most exclusive sets of the Old Town, houses will be coming tripping down Eastcott Hill and Prospect Hill and the Bath Road on their way to New Swindon. Rising on the railway boom, the more fortunate of the mechanics will climb the hill to greet them.'

In a poem written several years before his Swindon essay Betjeman described such houses as, 'brick-built breeding boxes of new souls'. To his subtle eye the little differences of detail and architectural gradations of Swindon houses from street to street and area to area reflect all the nuances of English social class. Bricks and mortar remain as mute evidence of the pretensions of their builders, and the aspirations of first and subsequent occupants. Observant pedestrians on their way down Victoria Road will notice such things; in particular they may spot the plaque recording the fact that Richard Jefferies lived for a year in one of the houses.

Jefferies was a man of the countryside, not the town, and to categorise him on the basis of his house as an aspiring middle-class Victorian seems somehow inadequate. Born at Coate in 1848 he was one of the last of thousands of Swindonians to be baptised at the old

Richard Jefferies.

parish church of Holy Rood (in January 1849) before its replacement by Christ Church in 1851. After a spell as a local journalist he supported himself and his family by writing novels and essays, until his premature death from tuberculosis in 1887. Interest in his work, never entirely extinguished, has revived from time to time, during the 1940s and 1970s, and now in the new millennium, with renewed interest in ecology and nature conservation, some of his books on country life and natural history are holding their place as classics of the genre. Opposition to recent building development at Coate, his old stamping ground, thrust him back into the local limelight as well. His output included work on local history, and we may claim him as Swindon's first historian, although this was not his forte. But,

The birthplace of Richard Jefferies at Coate, then an isolated hamlet east of Swindon, now a museum to his memory.

like Betjeman, he was interested in the sociology of the town, and his observations on Swindon in 1867 are astute.

Jefferies drew a distinction between 'the lower class of mechanics, especially the factory labourers', on the one hand, who were local men from the surrounding villages attracted to the works by higher wages; and the class of 'educated mechanics', on the other – well travelled, intelligent, eager to debate, read and learn. This latter group, 'in reality the protoplasm, or living matter, out of which modern society is evolved', were incomers to New Swindon, and their presence leavened the social life and character of the town. They ate meat and lived well, relatively speaking, but were not guilty of excesses; because they expected a regular income they tended to spend their money rather than save. This trait, in the eyes of Jefferies the farmer's son, was a grave character defect, but it resulted from a generous, liberal disposition, always ready to buy a friend a drink, take the family for a jaunt, or treat a daughter to a new dress. 'The mechanic does not set a value upon money in itself.'

This assessment accords precisely with F H Spencer's memory of his father, a precision engineer at the works who was descended from a Lancashire family of small landowners. A quiet, thoughtful man, 'with an unexhibited pride at the root of his nature', he had a passion for books, and for visiting abbeys and cathedrals to study their architecture. There was a second-hand piano in the house, and one of the children had a violin. But – and here Jefferies's stricture rings true – 'We were slightly in debt. The rent was always a few weeks in arrear, and there was an ancient butcher's bill incurred during the long stay of convalescent relatives in a distant past, which we gradually liquidated by occasional half-crowns.'

Spencer contrasts this household of culture, intellect and decency with the miserable condition of the rented house itself. This too has an echo in the observations of Jefferies. In one of his novels, *Greene Ferne Farm*, published in 1880, we follow a curate about his visits in 'Kingsbury', alias New Swindon. 'At the end of a new street hastily "run up cheap" and "scamped", they found a large black pool, once a pond in the meadow, now a slough of all imaginable filth, at whose precipitous edge the roadway stopped abruptly.' Upstairs in one of these 'scamped' six-roomed houses, with doors that warped and would not shut, they visited a young man recuperating from an accident at the works, lying on his bed in a sickly, fetid room in the middle of a summer day. He was one

Ornamental lettering on Sanford Street Boys School, built in 1881 (above), and Gilbert's Hill Infants and Girls School, Dixon Street of, 1880 and 1889 (below).

of the 'lower class of mechanics' arrived from a nearby village, and had been an under-shepherd. Now from his squalid surroundings he was staring out at lambs in a nearby field through a window that could not be made to open.

We suggested earlier that, during the doldrums of the late 1870s when this description was written, New Swindon had a respite, and took stock of its progress before beginning to organise itself as a proper town. In fact some urban trappings had already been in place for a number of years. Shops, schools, pubs and chapels sprang up throughout the town in the wake of new housing, and supplemented the medical, recreational and cultural facilities associated with the GWR. And both old and new towns had had their separate boards of health since 1864. The New Swindon Local Board organised gas street lamps, and began a rudimentary sewerage system. Although this was gradually improved and refined it continued for many years to demonstrate its shortcomings in various offensive ways, such as the slough of filth depicted by Jefferies. Later came a piped water supply from waterworks at Wroughton, and various public health and protection measures followed.

During the early years the two town boards refused to co-operate with each other, but gradually commonsense prevailed, and matters of

Radnor Street Cemetery, begun in 1880 and jointly funded by the two local boards. Now lovingly tended and researched, generations of Swindonians are buried here.

joint concern, such as firefighting, and the provision of a cemetery and an isolation hospital, were tackled together. During the building boom of the 1890s the conclusion became inevitable that Old and New Swindon should be governed together, and this was probably anticipated in the positioning of the New Swindon Local Board's offices at Regent Circus in 1891 – the Town Hall, as it became, was sited roughly halfway between the original nuclei of the two towns. During the 1890s amalgamation and incorporation as a borough became a burning local issue, and in 1897 the Privy Council was petitioned for Swindon to obtain its charter. On 9 November 1900, a little over sixty years after Gooch and Brunel had finished their picnic, the Borough of Swindon became a reality.

34 Faringdon Road, the Railway Village Museum, recreating life in Swindon, c.1900.

6
EVENING STAR AND SUNRISE

GASLIGHT IN THE LIVING ROOM, harmonium in the front parlour, and bowler hat hanging in the hall – the home life of the successful railway worker in about 1900 has been beautifully re-created at 34 Faringdon Road, the foreman's cottage which in 1980 was turned into the Railway Village Museum (run by the Mechanics Institution Trust, and open occasionally). James Hall, a second-generation Swindon railwayman, lived there in modest comfort with his wife and family, in the house which his parents had moved into when it was new and he was a child, forty years before in about 1860.

Within a short stroll from his back door was (or in 1900 would shortly be) a bewildering range of services and facilities provided by local government, 'the company', private enterprise and self-help. There were shops and pubs, a covered market and the mechanics' institute (with its enterprising range of social and cultural activities), churches and chapels, a hospital and swimming baths, and schools for the children. A theatre (the Queen's, later the Empire) had been built in 1898, some twenty working-men's clubs had opened between 1880 and 1900, professional football at the County Ground had begun in 1895, and there had been a local evening paper since 1882. A railway line connecting Old and New Swindon (part of the Midland and South Western Junction Railway from Cheltenham to Andover) was built in 1881-3. A few years' later, in 1903, the new borough council would take over the running of its schools, and also begin university extension lectures. During the same year an electricity works was built, and it generated power not only for electric

Samuel Loxton, a Bristol artist, drew Swindon scenes around 1900-1914, and these show some of the facilities by then available in the town, clockwise from top left: Electricity, including electric trams; the Mechanics Institute Library and Reading Room; the Technical School in Victoria Road; the Covered Market in Commercial Road.

street lighting, but also for a tramway system which started running services in 1904.

Everything – all these trappings of successful urban growth – was a product of the previous sixty years, and had grown up with the railway works, on which it all still ultimately depended for its existence. But during the twentieth century new themes emerged – the decline and fall of the works; the industries which came to replace them; and the overspill world of the suburbs.

The fate of the works may be gauged in statistics. The workforce had reached 14,000 by 1905, and peaked in 1925 at 14,369. In 1930 it was 11,500, and in 1939 10,500. After 1945 it remained fairly constant at about 10,000 until 1960, but had fallen to 8,000 in 1962, and 5,100 in 1967. A low point of 2,200 was reached in 1973, but thereafter it rose to 3,800 by 1980, before dropping to just over 1,000 before closure in 1986. It has been suggested that at the start of the century the GWR division based at Swindon, which was responsible for locomotives, carriages and wagons, as well as their drivers and firemen (a grand total of about

17,000 employees), was probably the largest undertaking in British, and perhaps European, industry at the time. With the opening of a new carriage store in 1938 the works reached their maximum geographical extent, more than 326 acres, including 79 acres roofed over.

Another way of looking at things is to consider the output of the works, and the legendary names of railway history responsible for designing and producing the famous locomotives built at Swindon. In 1901 G J Churchward, deputy and superintendent-elect, produced on a single sheet of paper the diagrams for six new types of locomotive, which employed a revolutionary boiler design. During his time in office (he retired as superintendent in 1921) five of these types went into production; they became the GWR's workhorses, and earned enviable

'King' class locomotives in front of the running shed, c.1924.

Aerial photograph of part of the railway works c.1924.

reputations for speed and reliability. Developments in carriage and wagon design also went on apace, and the ingenious designers and engineers in the works continued to show that they could turn their hand to any problem – in 1891 they had patented a cake-cutting machine for the annual children's fête, and in 1914 they built a pagoda-like advertising kiosk for use at agricultural shows, which still survives as a refreshment stall in the Town Gardens (see page 160). Churchward played an influential part too in the life of the town. He was the borough's mayor in the year of incorporation, and its first honorary freeman. After his retirement he continued to live in a house near the railway works until his death (run down by an express train while examining a loose rail) in 1933.

C B Collett, Churchward's successor, was responsible for developing many of the most famous classes of GWR locomotive, including 'Castles', 'Kings', 'Granges', 'Manors' and 'Halls'. His term of office (1922-41) also included the first experiments with diesel traction. On 1 January 1948 The GWR ceased to exist, and the nationalised British Railways took over the works, but steam locomotive production continued through the 1950s alongside new diesel-hydraulic units. The last steam locomotive to be built for British Railways emerged from the works on 18 March 1960, and was named 'Evening Star'. Diesel-hydraulic traction was phased out during the 1960s in favour of diesel-electric; this jeopardised Swindon's future, and by 1970 it seemed likely that British Rail Engineering Ltd (as it had become) would close the works. The gloom was premature, and it was not until 1985, while Swindon was preparing to celebrate the 150th anniversary of the founding of the GWR, that closure was announced, with effect from 26 March 1986. Commemoration gave way to anger, and the celebrations were abandoned.

'Evening Star', now preserved, seen here in 2015 (Peter Appleby, Wikimedia Commons).

'I had never been to Swindon before, and all I knew about it was that the Great Western Railway had its chief works there and that it made the best railway engines in the world.' So wrote J B Priestley when he visited the town in 1933. It was quite true, of course, and Swindon was proud of it. But civic pride had, by the 1930s, become tempered with a kind of malaise, which manifested itself in several ways. Priestley found the shops shoddy, the houses monotonous and the food in the eating-house dubious. As he trudged the damp, dark, autumnal town after dinner, and found it murky, with an unfriendly, shuttered look, he mused on 'these smaller industrial towns, where you can work but cannot really play'. Betjeman detected the same malaise in the new building of the inter-war years, which made Swindon, he said, look like any industrial suburb anywhere. And Kenneth Hudson, writing much later, during the 1960s, made himself very unpopular locally by suggesting that to the outside world, 'the name Swindon almost automatically conveyed the idea of somewhere out-of-date, small, mean and stick-in-the-mud,' and that this was, 'an important, if sad, part of the legacy of the railway town; it was a burden the town appeared to have to carry'. Hudson suggested a change of name to dispel the image, and provoked a storm of protest – yet Thamesdown Borough Council was less than a decade away.

An obvious explanation for the malaise is that it began when the works and the town stopped expanding at the phenomenal rate of the first sixty years. And it is precisely then, during the Edwardian years, that we first detect it, in a locally famous book, *Life in a Railway Factory*, by a locally famous author, Alfred Williams. Williams was a product of the mechanics' institute ethos of self-improvement for the working man by education. Poet, folksong collector, lover of the countryside, and student of ancient languages, he worked as a steam-hammerman at the works from 1893 until poor health ended his arduous career in 1914. He wrote his description of the works in 1911, but it was not published until 1915. It offers a detailed picture of the working environment, including all the dangers and hardships, the victimization and practical jokes. It is a powerful book by

Alfred Williams at his drop hammer in the railway works.

an embittered employee who, it must be admitted, is blatantly unsympathetic to the GWR. Much of the abuse and horseplay which he describes was harmless – apprentices, for instance, were misled by their older workmates into believing that they all had to be branded on one buttock with a large G, and on the other with a W (the company initials), using a hot iron stamp. But Williams also described a deteriorating relationship between shopfloor and management, as new machinery was introduced, bureaucracy increased, and the quest for greater efficiency imposed ever stiffer burdens on the workforce.

This increased tension in labour relations (by no means unique to Swindon at this time) which the disaffected Alfred Williams chronicled in his book is reflected also in the growth of union membership. A Swindon Trades Council was formed in 1891 to represent the various unions in the town, and it claimed that its membership of 1,000 in 1892 and 2,000 in 1903 had risen by 1917 to 10,000. The Trades Council put up candidates to local councils, including one man, Reuben George, who went on to become mayor and alderman of Swindon, and a county councillor, dying in 1936. A larger-than-life character, and champion of the Workers' Educational Association, he became one of Swindon's folk-heroes, along with the philanthropic rag-and-bone man, James 'Raggy' Powell, and David Murray John, town clerk from 1937 to 1974. In complete contrast to the shabby image Swindon may have had among outsiders, their wholehearted commitment to the town has given it a tangible civic pride and dignity which became a very notable feature of its twentieth-century history.

'Raggy' Powell, Reuben George and G J Churchward, caricatured in the 1920s.

As expansion and prosperity at the works became less dependable during and after the First World War, the borough and trades councils realised that Swindon had to diversify, and attract new industries into the town. Early arrivals – the clothing workshops already described, as well as Wills' tobacco factory in 1915, and Garrard Engineering in 1919 – were all chiefly employers of women, so did not provide a direct substitute for the railway works. In fact as numbers at the works began to decline during the 1930s many engineering workers found employment at Morris Motors in Cowley, Oxford, and commuted there from Swindon by train on a daily basis. Vickers Armstrong, who arrived at South Marston in 1937/8, was followed by other large engineering and electrical concerns during the Second World War, such as Plessey and R A Lister. Such were the employment opportunities in the town during the war, in fact, that immigration had to be limited, and Swindon was designated a closed area which civilians could not enter without permission.

Three new elements emerged after the war to complicate the process of expansion and diversification. First was the development of forward planning at local and national level. This meant that the opportunist piecemeal growth of the town in response to the needs of employers was a thing of the past. From now on its course would be master-minded. Second was the problem that Swindon, within its existing boundaries, was full up, and any further expansion would encroach on the neighbouring local authority – Highworth Rural District Council – and affect Wiltshire County Council. There was a long-standing antipathy between Swindon and the rest of Wiltshire, which grew worse after 1974, when many local government services were transferred to the county. 'Trowbridge' (Wiltshire's county town) became a dirty word in Swindon, and periodical outbreaks of hostility continued until 1997, when the Swindon area achieved the status of a unitary authority, and so became largely independent of the county. Third was government policy, which at first favoured the creation of new towns, but after 1951 preferred the controlled growth of existing centres as 'overspill' towns. Swindon was designated a London overspill town on 25 June 1952, and this had a profound effect on its subsequent development.

The industrial and employment consequences, which we should look at first, were that numerous engineering, electrical, scientific and

One of many companies to move their major offices to Swindon was W H Smith. Their Greenbridge office block of 1965-7 is now (2023) under threat of demolition with the site to be developed for housing. This photograph dates from 2005.

distributive companies opened plants in and around Swindon during the 1950s and 1960s. They included one, Pressed Steel, which by 1965 had a larger workforce at its Stratton premises than the railway works. By 1970, encouraged in particular by the borough council's vigorous promotion of itself to potential employers, there were over 35,000 manufacturing jobs in Swindon. Many were located in units on council-initiated trading and industrial estates. Expansion continued during the 1970s, although the main growth now was in service and white-collar industries. A temporary check during the early 1980s was followed by a dramatic upturn in Swindon's fortunes, especially in what were then being called the 'sunrise' industries, of computers, electronics and information technology. The startling architecture of Swindon's 1980s new image greets the visitor along the western access road from the motorway – the motorway (opened in 1971) which was one of its chief progenitors.

Hand in hand with the town's policy of diversified employment has been the suburbanization of Swindon, and this is the final theme

A futuristic office building at Windmill Hill Business Park, close to the M4 motorway. The windmill was re-erected here from Chiseldon in 1988 (Roger Ogle).

Arclite House at Peatmoor, West Swindon, opened in 1999, has housed several businesses and suffered periods of disuse (photographed in 2005).

in our summary of twentieth-century history. In chapter five we left Swindon in around 1900 at the point where the two towns had coalesced, and redbrick had sprawled haphazardly around them in most directions. But Swindon's Victorian housing development was not really suburban, rather it was a series of small accretions and piecemeal infillings, often on rather cramped sites. This process continued until 1914, with new housing concentrated on the Okus, Kingshill and quarry areas west of Old Town, the Broad Street district near the station, and north of the tracks at Gorse Hill and Even Swindon. After the First World War Swindon began to march out into the countryside. (You may find it helpful to read the rest of this chapter alongside chapter 11, where the suburbs are further described, with a map.)

During the 1920s and 1930s, here as everywhere, there were two types of housing, council and private. In general terms council houses were sturdier, built to better specifications, and more imaginatively positioned on estates. The overriding concern for private housebuilders and occupiers, rooted in class snobbery, was that their houses should not look like council houses; in other respects economies were made, and this included so-called ribbon development along existing main roads, which saved expense on building the infrastructure of estate roads and services. Swindon expanded northwards, with a council estate at Pinehurst, and private housing at Rodbourne. The Pinehurst estate was laid out on a circular plan by one of the pioneers of the garden city movement, Sir Raymond Unwin (although he was not responsible for the design of the

Early council housing of the 1920s around Pinehurst Circle, now a century old.

houses), and its tree-named streets were gradually built up between the wars. In addition to the Rodbourne estate private housing ribboned along the main roads radiating from Old Town. In 1928 much of the ancient parish of Rodbourne Cheney was absorbed within the borough boundary, and part of Stratton St Margaret was taken as well.

Swindon's population in 1901, we recall, was 45,000, and this had been a ninefold increase during the previous fifty years. By 1951 it had reached 69,000 – a substantial increase, but on nothing like the scale of the nineteenth century. Decade by decade between 1901 and 1951 the average growth was less than 10%, a comfortable rate of expansion which these suburban adventures could readily accommodate. But after 1945, and especially after the London overspill decision in 1952, the rate of growth increased again, with a consequent need for carefully planned suburban expansion. Between 1951 and 1961 another 23,000 people came to live in Swindon, nearly as many in ten years as in the previous fifty. But they were only the tip of an anticipated iceberg. Plans produced during the 1960s envisaged growth to 180,000, 200,000, 230,000, even 400,000 by the end of the century. The 200,000 estimate, suggested in 1968, became the accepted target.

Until the 1952 decision, Swindon's post-war housing effort had been concentrated, as before, to the north of the town. To these years principally belong the suburbs of Moredon and Penhill. But from 1952 a massive expansion to the east began. Walcot East and Walcot West

London overspill housing and high-rise flats of the 1950s on the Park South estate.

As Swindon expanded eastwards traffic management became a problem, and at one junction this was solved by the borough engineer, Norman Pritchard, who devised a road layout of five small roundabouts clustered around one large one. Inaugurated in 1972 (over fifty years ago!) locals have always negotiated it with ease, but it strikes terror into newcomers, and for Swindon the Magic Roundabout has achieved fame and notoriety.

came first, separated not only by a new dual-carriageway road, Queen's Drive of 1953, but also by the English class system, which was still endeavouring to distinguish between council and private houses. Next came private housing at Lawn, and council housing at Park North and South. And with them, in the early 1960s, Swindon's boundaries were full up again, and further expansion had to encroach on its neighbours. Meanwhile those neighbours were themselves growing rapidly. The two rural districts bordering Swindon (Cricklade and Wootton Bassett, and Highworth) grew by a total of nearly 20,000 population between 1951 and 1966, and one parish, Stratton St Margaret, returned a population of 19,400 at the 1971 census, which was larger than most Wiltshire towns.

The key planning document of the 1960s, the so-called 'Silver Book', spawned further suburban housing and industrial expansion. Initially this was concentrated to the east, at Liden, Nythe, Covingham, Dorcan and Eldene, where gradual infilling took place up to the line of the Stratton St Margaret by-pass (our old friend the Roman road). But during the 1980s an entirely new area was opened up west of

Typical 1980s estate housing, with ample green space, at Ramleaze, West Swindon.

Fleming Way in 2020, before its ongoing (2023) transformation. Named after a notable footballing hero, Harold Fleming, and following the line of the North Wilts Canal, it was part of a widespread movement adopted in many towns and cities during the 1960s to remove vehicular traffic from shopping streets, leaving them free and safe for pedestrians. Beneath Fleming Way an underpass, which was closed in August 2023 (see page 175), linked The Parade to the bus and rail stations.

Swindon, and this was developed as a self-contained community, with its own facilities. Meanwhile radical changes were taking place in the town centre, as Victorian cottages were demolished to make way for pedestrianised shopping precincts. Here the inspiration was an influential report by the distinguished town planner, Sir Colin Buchanan, published in 1963, which recommended segregating traffic and pedestrians by removing cars from town centre shopping streets.

Opposite page: Street market flourishing without traffic in The Parade.

7
NO MEAN CITY?

AS PART OF HER GOLDEN JUBILEE commemorations in 2002 the late Queen Elizabeth graciously agreed not to grant Swindon the status of a city. She had reached the same decision two years earlier when celebrating the millennium. It was another sad day for Swindon's not-to-be citizens, mitigated only by the news that their arch-rival Reading had been similarly rejected. It was long odds – only one out of the twenty-six applications from English towns could be successful – and city status is, after all, purely honorific. But success would have set a kind of royal seal of approval on how much Swindon had achieved in the previous decades, and failure was, well, failure – especially when set against Her Majesty's stated criteria, which included historical features, regional and national significance and a forward-looking attitude. Subsequent aspirations to city status have been no more successful, and Swindon remains a town within a borough. Perhaps conurbation would be a more appropriate description, for a place whose population is creeping up to the quarter-million. 'Town' seems wholly inadequate.

Swindon at work, in the 1980s, was a mix of manufacturing, service and so-called 'sunrise' industries. At the turn of the millennium there was still this mix, though new ingredients had been added and the quantities had changed. In parallel with national trends, manufacturing industries were in decline, but Honda's arrival at South Marston in 1989,

The Murray John Tower, 22 storeys and 270 feet high, Swindon's signature landmark, was built in 1975-6. It commemorates a local hero, David Murray John (1908-74), town clerk from 1938 until his death, and the architect of modern Swindon. When the borough lost its autonomy in 1974 under local government reorganisation, he was already ailing, and died on his 66th birthday, allegedly of a broken heart.

The innovative Renault building in West Swindon, photographed in 2005 when disused.

and the Japanese company's major investments in new plant in 2001 and 2012, seemed for three decades to have assured for Swindon a long-term career as a car-making centre of international significance. This dream ended in 2019 with an announcement, and the plant closed in 2021. It was only the biggest example of many other industrial arrivals and departures, some of which have left interesting buildings to find other uses (Renault's Spectrum in West Swindon, opened in 1982 and abandoned in 2001; Arclite at Peatmoor, mostly empty from 2004 to 2015; Motorola off Thamesdown Drive, closed in 2010).

Financial institutions, notably Allied Dunbar and Nationwide, came here in the 1970s and have stayed. Zurich Insurance, successor to Allied Dunbar, opened its Unity Place office for more than 1,000 staff in the town centre in 2023; Nationwide moved its headquarters to a greenfield site on Swindon's southern outskirts in 1992, and has become the town's largest employer. Butter, books, pills, mobile phones, car and computer bits, oil, railway services, compact discs, electricity, and a host of other requirements – as like as not the producing or supplying company had its head office in Swindon in 2000, and many still do. And alongside these captains of commerce a new species arrived, the quango. Following on from the government research councils, who migrated here during the 1970s, the National Monuments Record Centre (now

Zurich Insurance building, Unity Place, 2023, a note of confidence in the town centre.

part of Historic England) came in 1994, and was joined in 2005, as eco-friendly next-door neighbour on the railway works site, by Heelis, the headquarters of the National Trust.

Bravo Swindon! On the scale of social kudos hosting the National Trust probably ranks higher than achieving city status. But, as in the

Heelis, ecological headquarters of the National Trust, built on part of the former railway works site, and opened in 2005. Mrs William Heelis, aka Beatrix Potter, was one of the Trust's pioneer benefactors.

19th century, so in the 21st, new employers mean new patterns of employment. Three points should be made which affect Swindon's significance and attitude. First, a considerable though unquantified proportion of the new workforce does not live in or feel any allegiance to Swindon, but commutes – in many cases from considerable distances. Second, the balance of male and female employment has undoubtedly shifted, offering a welcome and healthy equality. And third, many of the new employers are multi-national companies, offering Swindon its chance to shine on the global stage, but also leaving it susceptible to globally distant boardroom politics.

Earning it is one thing, spending it is another. The town centre's pedestrian streets and Brunel plaza, so radical in the 1970s, were looking tired by the 1990s, and ready for the facelift they received in 1995-7. A new covered market was created and, near the site of its predecessor, a large department store was built by a high-class chain. Shortly afterwards, in 1998, Swindon's home-grown department store, McIlroys, which had been trading in Regent Street since the Victorian period, closed its doors and was swiftly demolished. Plans under way in 2005 envisaged, not so much cosmetic surgery for the town centre, more a heart and lung transplant, as new vital organs were to replace the old, with fanciful and contemporary names, Hub, Arena, Campus, Promenade, Exchange.

Two images from 2005: the roof of the covered market, in 2023 disused and deteriorating; and the entrance to the Brunel shopping centre, which by 2023 was almost empty of shops.

Some of these materialised. The new Swindon Central Library opened in 2008. Its neighbour, the 1960s Swindon College looking down on Regent Circus, was closed in 2006 and demolished in 2012, to be replaced by a cinema, superstore and restaurant complex in 2015. Wharf Green, next to the Brunel Centre, was improved in 2008, and began to be used in 2012 for open-air events, with a street market nearby in now pedestrianised Havelock Street. The area between the railway station and Fleming Way filled with tall office blocks, centred on Newbridge Square. Other aspirations foundered, such as the proposed museum below Theatre Square, or in 2023 remain on the drawing board.

Against the optimism and ambition must be set the reality that Swindon town centre, including large parts of the Brunel Centre, are

Swindon Central Library, built adjoining the Town Hall in 2008, and replacing long worn-out temporary library buildings on the same site.

Newbridge Square, between the railway station and the town centre. It replaces streets of Victorian terraced housing built by the Cheltenham and Gloucester Building Society, and takes its name from a bridge over the North Wilts Canal nearby.

wished and striven for, proved neither panacea nor utopia. The cost of restructuring, shortfalls in government-imposed spending levels, and critical reports of under-performance, all dented the slogan 'proud to be Swindon'. In response to its problems the New Swindon Company, an urban regeneration partnership, was formed in 2002 to revitalise the town centre and, having foundered, re-formed as Forward Swindon in 2010. The years since 2008, particularly, have been very lean, the council (like many others) lurching from one financial crisis to another, as central government support has been progressively withdrawn, so that the council has been forced to cut services and sell off assets. Despite the austerity, perceived by many as politically motivated, Swindon's demographic had shifted sufficiently by 2010 from its proud working-class image to elect two Conservative MPs.

Meanwhile Swindon has continued to expand. The vision of the 'Silver Book' of 1968 was that suburban development should take place to the east (the Eldene and Liden area and South Marston), to

The Link Centre of 1984-5 at Westlea, the equivalent town centre of West Swindon.

West Swindon is notable for championing public art, and no piece is more memorable than the statue of Swindon native Diana Dors outside the Shaw Ridge leisure complex and cinema.

the west (Toothill, Westlea, Freshbrook and Shaw), and to the north (the so-called Haydon sector); and that within each should be built a series of 'urban villages', or neighbourhoods. Though endlessly modified as to timing, extent, responsibility and finance, and the subject of numerous subsequent reports, the actual geography of Swindon's suburbs turned out much as the 1968 planners envisaged. Eldene and Liden were built in the early 1970s, and work began at West Swindon, with the creation of Toothill between 1974 and 1979. A planning inquiry sanctioned development of the other West Swindon neighbourhoods in 1978, but because of recession and financial restraints, housebuilding proceeded much more slowly than had been envisaged, and took nearly twenty years to complete.

Development of the Haydon sector, to the north and west of Swindon's older suburbs at Moredon and Penhill, was politically contentious during the 1980s, and a protracted and unsettled period ensued, of planning applications, building consortia, revised forecasts and planning inquiries, before construction began in 1995. An orbital road, Thamesdown Way, was built to act as a conduit, linking the 'villages' to each other, to their North Swindon District Centre (the Orbital Retail Park), and to the outside world. New communities with anodyne names – Abbey Meads, Priory Vale, Taw Hill – began to establish themselves, quite different in conception from those in West Swindon. The zeitgeist now was retro, so that anyone venturing between Thamesdown Way and Tadpole Lane will find a pastiche of every imaginable (and unimaginable) style of domestic architecture cheek by jowl, from Cotswold cottage to Regency crescent.

Contrasting neighbours in Eastbury Way, North Swindon.

With the Silver Book's vision almost realised, new planning battle lines were drawn. Attention turned south, beyond Old Town and Coate Water towards the thick blue line of the M4 motorway, and the areas of farmland in between, dubbed Swindon's 'front garden'. By 2006 the developers had plunged deep into medieval history and discovered the hapless Wichel, who had once farmed and had his '*stowe*' (or place) there. East Wichel was built over first, and then Middle Wichel after 2010, where the old Wilts and Berks Canal was restored and became a feature. In 2014 work began building houses between Coate Water and the Great Western Hospital – on the very fields immortalised by Richard Jefferies.

There was more that could be built over in the north too, despite protests from the previous wave of new settlers. Tadpole Farm and Ridgeway Farm (both 2012) and St Andrew's Ridge (2014) gained approval, so that there were calls for a new link road to service the extra population. But that, it was claimed, would open floodgates to more new houses towards Purton and Cricklade (and outside the borough boundary, in Wiltshire), and the plans were dropped. Attention turned to the east, towards South Marston and Wanborough, where approval for

The northern and southern limits of Swindon's suburbs, as of the 2020s. Tadpole Village takes its name from a Blunsdon farm and lane; More than 7km south Middle Wichel, with its spectacular bridge over the restored Wilts and Berks Canal, is named after its Saxon owner.

the Swindon and Cricklade Railway, the designation of a nature reserve at Haydon Meadow and a scheduled ancient monument on Groundwell Ridge, all suggest that Swindon, if not pioneering in, is at least conforming to the prevailing climate of environmental sensitivity.

Beginning in 1976, when the first couple moved into their new home in West Swindon, and repeated in 1996 in North Swindon, the dynamic has changed. No longer is Swindon a town with ever-burgeoning suburbs; it has become three large towns – near neighbours, admittedly, but socially quite separate. And there are others, still in embryo. Wichelstowe, in 2023 as I write, is partly formed, the Eastern Villages are still gestating. What does that mean for the older Swindon, which this book has tried to decode? Its centre, as one walks through, seems poor – closed shops and arcades, struggling businesses, struggling people. Not such a far cry from the railway town that Kenneth Hudson

Lydiard House within its park, purchased by Swindon Corporation in 1943.

was striving to understand over 50 years ago when he researched his sociological study of Swindon 'at the 100,000 mark', although the population has more than doubled since then. His book, *An Awkward Size for a Town*, published in 1967, described in great detail the living standards and aspirations of 1960s Swindonians. The dowdy image of the railway terraces had not then been shaken off, the shopping malls of the town centre were not complete, the Wyvern Theatre had not been built, the 'hi-tech' industries were decades away, the railway works were still a powerful force. Replying to a questionnaire about his ambitions a sixth-former replied in terms of the initials he wanted to see after his name – BSc, PhD, FRS, OBE, 'and having made this clear, said he doubted if Swindon was going to be big enough to hold him'. He will be long retired by now. Has Swindon thrown off its awkwardness, and become big enough in significance and attitude (as well as geographically) to have held him? Did he achieve his ambitions? And has Swindon?

The Golden Lion.

Strolling around Swindon

IF YOU HAVE READ my book this far you will have been given most of the clues you need to decode Swindon, In the four chapters that make up this second part we shall walk together around Old Town and the Railway complex, as one would expect, but also explore the area in between – which in my somewhat idiosyncratic opinion is just as interesting. Then, for all but the most intrepid walkers, we shall use buses, bikes or (if you must) cars to explore Swindon's suburbs – the older ones and then the more recent.

But a word of warning. There is plenty that has gone wrong with modern Swindon, starved as it has been of government funding over several decades. Although processes, policies and consequences are valid subjects for the historian to study, these are not the concern of this part of the book, and we shall not be judgmental. As observers and decoders we are only concerned with what we can see, and with understanding how it came to be as it is.

Throughout these chapters instructions about the route are given in italics. The paragraph(s) of description which follow usually relate to features visible at points along this part of the route, so should be read while carrying out the instruction. The maps are based on large-scale Ordnance Survey plans published around 1900, on to which the route has been added in colour. Pedestrian crossings and road crossings with dropped kerbs are used wherever possible, and possible difficulties and alternatives for wheelchair users are described.

Old Swindon corn exchange of 1864-6, 'spectacularly derelict', as described in a 2021 architectural guide.

8
THE HILLTOP TOWN

TO UNDERSTAND SWINDON before the railway we must begin in Old Town, loitering in the unprepossessing small car park off the High Street facing the derelict Town Hall. If you are an old Swindonian you will remember this building as the Locarno ballroom; and if you are not you can probably still see why.

This is the former market place of a small medieval town and, as such, was crucial to the community's existence and prosperity. Swindon is one of hundreds of examples of a small town planned and laid out by a landowner during the twelfth and thirteenth centuries (around 1260 in Swindon's case), in the hope that they could turn farmland or waste into something more profitable, by attracting traders and craftsmen and charging them rent and tolls. To do this not only was a market place essential, to sell their goods and buy their food, but also plots laid out along streets, where they could build their homes, with their workshops and backyards. High Street and Newport Street (the clue is in the name – 'port' means market) are probably the earliest components of the new town's street plan, and the houses that line them, though much later, occupy the plots on which the first settlers had their premises. Those fronting High Street are long and narrow, as we shall see when we walk around, but Newport Street was humbler, and the rear yards of its cottages much shorter.

Some of these speculative new trading places were built on entirely new sites, but most, like Swindon, were adjacent to an existing village, and we shall look for that shortly. Sometimes the speculation paid off and a large town developed and thrived. Others were failures from the start. Swindon seems to be one of the many that did manage to become a town in a small way, but never really prospered, or not at least until the 17th century. So none of the buildings we see around are medieval, but the streets and open spaces in this area go back to Swindon's urban origins.

After relative obscurity for several centuries Swindon's market only really began to flourish after it was revived in 1626, and thereafter it competed with Highworth as the principal cattle market in north-east Wiltshire. There were more people living here too, as the fine building stone beneath the surface of the hill began to be exploited. This revitalised market place had a covered market cross in the centre, perhaps like the one that survives at Malmesbury, but this was demolished in 1793.

In common with many other towns at the time, Swindon in the 19th century tried to make its market more attractive for farmers and corn dealers. A market house was begun on the south side of the square in 1852, replacing a depot for long-distance waggons (which the railway had made redundant). This market house is the classical building, of which only the shell remains, seen to the right of the tower, but although its upper floor was used for its intended purpose as a Town Hall, the ground floor never became a covered market, and its arches were filled in for shops. Instead a new corn exchange with an Italianate tower was built to the left of it in 1864-6. After some fifty years the building became a skating rink and later a cinema, ballroom and bingo hall. The motto over the door, 'Blessed be the Lord who daily loadeth us with benefits' is perhaps more appropriate to a corn exchange than to bingo.

Opposite these buildings of Bath and local stone, on the north side is a smart brick house of the 1770s, Square House, a reminder of Georgian Swindon's aspirations to gentility . And to the east runs Dammas Lane, which was formerly built up with small houses. The name is supposed to derive from damsons, as the lane led to the manor house orchards. The adjacent Saxon Court, a modern housing development, occupies the area in which Saxon huts were discovered and excavated, and so may represent the centre of a much earlier settlement which preceded the medieval town.

1 *Face the corn exchange and walk past it along High Street to its right, and beyond the modern building, noting Newport Street joining at the mini-roundabout. Turn left and walk across the car park to the lane called The*

THE HILLTOP TOWN 151

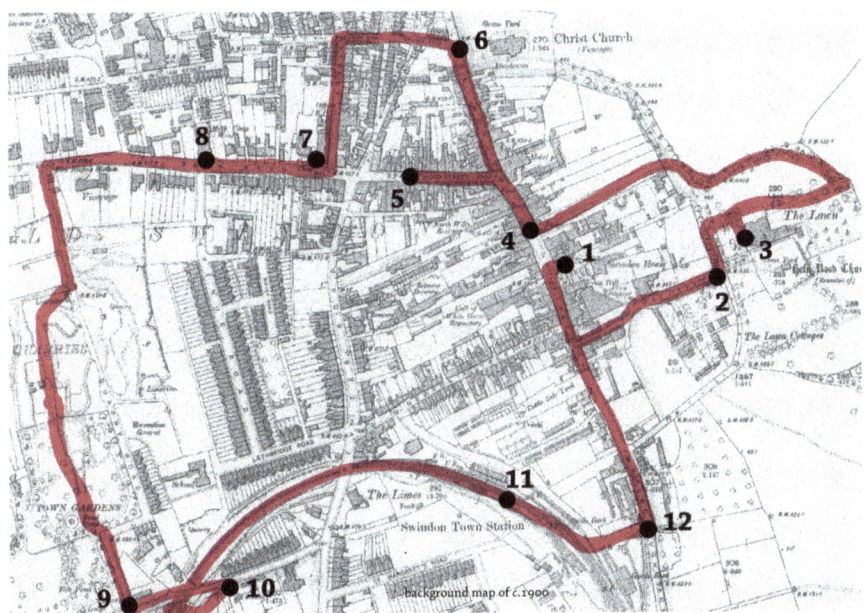

Planks. Walk along this lane, past the auction rooms, until the lane bears right in front of a tree-lined grassed area. **2** *Here turn left and walk up the path into the public park known as The Lawn. Explore the remains of the manor house gardens adjoining the locked churchyard of Holy Rood on your right. (Wheelchair users will find it easier to turn right from the Market Square into High Street, and then turn right again between ornamental gate piers along the tree-lined path to The Lawn. The churchyard is away to the right.)*

As soon as we have left High Street and Newport Street we have moved from the medieval planned town in pursuit of the older village. The Planks is supposedly derived from a dialect name for flagstones, and it leads towards the site of a mill demolished in about 1860. The mill, a vital component of village life, which stood below the churchyard, was fed by a spring called Church Well and turned by an extremely large overshot water wheel standing more than thirty feet high. The spring was also

The Planks.

Sunken garden at The Lawn.

used as a water supply, and still feeds the lakes which lie at the southern end of The Lawn, below the church.

'The Lawn' is the name given not only to the area of wooded landscape parkland which separates Old Swindon from the twentieth-century suburbs of Lawn, Park and Walcot, but was also used for the manor house which stood within it until it was demolished in 1952. A sunken garden survives with balustrades, which lay immediately west of the house. The house itself was of brick and stone, and rather similar in style to a surviving house (42, Cricklade Street) which we shall see presently. The Lawn was earlier called Swindon House, and was until 1931 the home of the Goddard family, manorial owners of High Swindon. Although we do not have very early maps or other documentation, we can surmise that this mansion occupied the site of the manor (or demesne) house of Swindon's medieval owners before the planned town was created in the thirteenth century. If so, and by analogy with other places, here and around the church would have been the early village, which had either disappeared by the time The Lawn was created, or was swept away when the area was landscaped for the mansion's grounds and parkland.

The adjoining (locked) churchyard contains the chancel and part of the nave arcade of Holy Rood Church. This was Swindon's parish church from the middle ages until 1851, when Christ Church was completed. The author Richard Jefferies was baptised here in 1849. By this date it consisted of a mixture of medieval work and eighteenth-century repairs, which included a new brick tower. But the whole structure was in poor repair – 'hopelessly out of condition, and there being really nothing

The gazebo.

worth restoring', according to an author who remembered it very well – so that the new church was built, and Holy Rood was allowed to deteriorate. The tower was demolished, and re-erected to its original proportions as a kind of gazebo on a mound not far away; the chancel was restored in 1964.

View from The Lawn.

The Lawn's parkland is a pleasant place for a stroll, with its lakes and trees and avenue, from the far end of which there is a long view eastwards across the suburbs of Walcot, Park, Lawn and beyond, which are explored below in chapter 11.

3 *From the churchyard area walk towards the brick gazebo tower, and about halfway between them you will encounter a substantial path. Turn left along this and follow it to the exit from The Lawn, which is by a long avenue of young oak trees (planted in 1992 to replace storm-damaged trees). This emerges into High Street between a pair of ornamental gatepiers. Stop at this point to examine the architecture of the street.*

As you approach the High Street you are leaving the Goddard family's park and estate by the main entrance, which originally had lodge houses on each side, as well as the surviving gatepiers. But you are also walking the length of one of the long, narrow plots laid out along High Street in the 13th century when the town was being developed.

Gatepier at The Lawn's former entrance.

The row of buildings opposite, along the western side of the street, dates from the sixteenth to the nineteenth century, and is typical north Wiltshire small-town architecture. They reflect the upturn in Swindon's fortunes which we noticed earlier. These premises also have long plots

Bell Inn.

running back behind them, the legacy of their medieval origins, with gateways from the street giving access to some of them. Looking at the row from left to right, the Bell has a Victorian facade of 1878 with a huge bell, but retains traces of a 17th-century or earlier galleried inn behind. Four doors along, at No.16, notice 'GH' and the date 1631 on the rainwater heads. Old Town Court proclaims 'Bowly Brewer' above its semicircular arch. Bowly during the 1860s took over the North Wilts Brewery, behind High Street, from John Henry Harding Sheppard, who went into property development in New Swindon, as we shall see in Chapter 10. No.4, Eastcott House, is the former King of Prussia Inn, and may date from the 17th century; the corner shop has a date of 1708 and the letters 'MH'.

4 *From the gatepiers turn right along High Street, and cross by the pedestrian crossing. Continue to the corner and venture halfway along Wood Street as far as* **5** *the King's Arms, and then back again to the junction. Now walk straight on down the hill until you find yourself opposite the entrance to Christ Church. But read the following paragraphs as you go.*

Opposite the junction with Wood Street stands Old Swindon's principal inn, the Goddard Arms. The site had earlier been occupied by one of the town's manor houses, and then a thatched inn called the Crown. The present creeper-clad building dates from about 1815. So we are still in the world of the Georgian hilltop town, before the railway has arrived. But turn the corner into Wood Street and we find a Swindon transformed. Here is a successful Victorian shopping street, brimming with extravagant decoration – just look at the King's Arms!

All this show derives from the prosperity which accrued to Old Town traders during the mid-nineteenth century, before New Swindon

King's Arms.

had developed its own proper infrastructure of shopping streets. A directory of 1848 claimed that Old Swindon's shops were 'assuming an appearance equal to those of Bath and Cheltenham'. But a few years earlier it had been lined by poor labourers' thatched cottages and blacksmith's forges, producing intolerable noise and smoke, according to Richard Jefferies, who remembered it as a child. It was sometimes called Blacksmith's Street, or alternatively Windmill Street, because of a windmill which occupied a site near the King's Arms. Back to the corner, and the former Wilts and Dorset Bank building of 1884 occupies the site of Blackford's butcher's shop. Before Wood Street's transformation members of the Blackford family had been champion backsword players, a game which involved clubbing an opponent's head with a wooden stick until the blood ran one inch.

Beyond the Wood Street junction the road continues northward as Cricklade Street, although its old name was Brock Hill. It soon begins to descend the hillside, and a long view over Swindon's northern suburbs opens up. Until a fatal coaching accident in the early 19th century the road was carried more abruptly over the brow of the hill, on a level with the present pavement on the Christ Church side. After the accident the gradient was eased for the safety of wheeled vehicles, but not without complaints from the owner of the grand house at the top of the hill. This, No. 42

42 Cricklade Street.

Cricklade Street, is generally regarded as the finest piece of domestic architecture in Swindon. Sir John Betjeman called it 'one of the most distinguished town houses in Wiltshire'. It was built in 1729, and was occupied as a private house by members of leading Swindon families, including Harding and Vilett, before becoming the county court and offices.

Further down the hill an inscription records a bequest by Alexander Anderson which paid for a group of four almshouses next to the churchyard in 1877. Christ Church was designed by Sir George Gilbert Scott in Midlands Decorated style, and was opened in 1851. The hillside site was donated by Ambrose Goddard, lord of the manor, and the lofty spire, which is such a prominent feature of the Swindon townscape, was copied from the genuinely medieval spire at Buckworth

Christ Church and Anderson almshouses.

near Huntingdon. 'So new, so high, so pure, so broach'd, so tall', it presides over the peal of ten bells celebrated in verse by Betjeman.

6 *Opposite Christ Church turn left into Church Road, which later becomes Union Row. When this emerges into the main road (Victoria Road) turn left, cross by the pedestrian crossing, and make your way back up towards Old*

THE HILLTOP TOWN

Town. At the T-junction and mini-roundabout at the top of Victoria Road follow the pavement around to the right, so that you find yourself outside **7** *Apsley House, the former Swindon Museum. Continue along the right hand side of Bath Road until you reach the Methodist Church, but stopping to read the following commentary as you go.*

The siting of Christ Church on Brock Hill must have improved the status of what had been the poor end of the town. A street of meagre cottages called Little London ran down from the west end of Wood Street to join Brock Hill where it bends shortly below Christ Church. This is no longer built up, and now has the appearance of a back alley. Church Road crosses it, and then meets Albert Street, which retains some of its 1840s stone cottages, but not its notorious pub, the Rhinoceros Inn, which stood at this crossing until it was demolished in 1963.

With Wood Street and Christ Church we are beginning to see the changes in Old Town that resulted from the growing presence during the 1840s and 1850s of the railway community below. This mingling of new replacing old will be our main theme from now on. Albert Street and Victoria Street (as the upper end of Victoria Road was originally known) are the most tangible evidence of this. When you have crossed the pedestrian crossing in Victoria Road look back across the road, and you will see a quite distinguished terrace of 1850s stone houses (as opposed to the later and meaner brick houses beyond the Union Row turning). On No.93 at first floor level a plaque records that this was the home of Richard Jefferies, the Wiltshire naturalist and country writer, from 1875-7.

93 Victoria Road, with plaque to Richard Jefferies.

Walking up Victoria Road to its junction it is important to realise that, despite its present importance as the main road between Old and New Swindon, this link was not established until about 1875, as the towns began to coalesce. This growing together will be one of our main themes in chapter 10. Earlier

Bath Terrace.

ways up and down the hill were by Brock Hill and Little London, which we have just seen, and by Eastcott Hill, which we shall encounter later. Victoria Street in the 1850s and 1860s ended merely in a footpath across fields, by way of Prospect (beyond the present BBC Wiltshire building).

At the top of Victoria Road, as our footpath leads us round the corner into Bath Road, it is time to take stock. Swindon's medieval street plan was roughly a square of four streets. We have seen the end of Newport Street, the square's southern side, and we have walked along High Street, the eastern side, and part of Wood Street, the northern side. Now we are at the north-western corner, and the western side is represented by Devizes Road. This was known as Short Hedge until the 19th century, and was not built up to any great extent.

Regency house in Bath Road.

But now we are standing at pre-Victorian Swindon's growth point. Between the 1820s and 1850 housing had begun to creep from this junction southward along Devizes Road, northward (as we have just seen) along Victoria Street, and westward along what was then called The Sands, but is now Bath Road. Among the first of the new arrivals (probably by 1830) was Apsley House, which was home to Swindon Museum from 1930 until 2020. A larger and later development was Bath Terrace, the long row of shops opposite the top of Victoria Road.

Bath Road Methodist church.

Bath Road is the fashionable nineteenth-century extension to Old Swindon, and its houses display a pleasing variety of styles, using brick, local stone, and occasionally Bath stone. After Apsley House the earliest are the attractive brick houses (now offices) with cast-iron porches, Nos. 8-14; they date from about 1835, and so are pre-railway. But on the other side of the road, and further along on both sides, the villas are decidedly Victorian, and mostly date from the 1850s and 1860s. The chapel was opened in 1880, and replaced earlier buildings in the Planks.

8 *Now cross the road by the pedestrian crossing just beyond the chapel and continue along Bath Road (away from Old Town) until you reach Quarry Road. Turn left down Quarry Road and, after about 100 yards, enter the Town Gardens by iron gates on your right.*

Entrance to the Town Gardens.

Aviary and pond, Town Gardens.

Just as the original village community, and indeed the nascent small town, needed a mill and a church, so it needed agricultural land to cultivate for its food. Here, now occupied by the Town Gardens and surrounding residential streets, was the area of medieval Swindon's open arable land. But from the 17th century quarries were opened up in parts of this field, at first to win Purbeck limestone, and later the Portland stone with which much of Old Swindon is built. Quarrying declined in the later 19th century, and the Town Gardens were laid out as a public park in 1894. Their design makes full and attractive use of the different levels which resulted from quarrying activities, and they are a delight to explore. Near the bandstand is a polygonal refreshment kiosk. This was built by the GWR in Swindon works in 1914 for advertising purposes at local shows, and later sold to the borough council.

The GWR refreshment kiosk.

9 *Make your way through the park to its main entrance in Westlecot Road. Cross the road and turn left. Walk along Westlecot Road until you reach the parapet of a railway bridge, and see the deep railway cutting below you. Unless you are a wheelchair user (in which case continue along Westlecot and Springfield Roads, left into Croft Road, right into Newport Street, and so back to the start), turn right into Bowling Green Lane, and immediately you will find a* **10** *footpath sloping down the side of the cutting. On the floor of the cutting turn back sharp right, so that you walk under the railway bridge. Continue in the cutting, and under another bridge, until you emerge into a small industrial estate.*

The path leading down to the railway cutting.

As we return to our starting point we are witnessing the

final stages of Old Swindon as a separate town – it was amalgamated with New Swindon in 1900. Springfield Road, where we descend into the railway cutting, had been part of the lane which led from the former quarries, and was just starting to be built up with houses during the 1890s; Westlecot Road and many residential streets further west would follow shortly.

We are walking along part of the Midland and South Western Junction Railway line, which ran from Cheltenham to Southampton. This portion, with a station known as Swindon Town (the mainline station was then called Swindon Junction), was opened in 1881-2, and closed in 1961. The station itself was approached from Newport Street and the nearby Steam Railway pub commemorates it; the site of the station has become the industrial estate, and a mural painting reminds us of its former use. While walking in the cutting look for exposures of Swindon stone.

The ram at Dewell Mews.

11 *Take a left turn (Dewell Mews) out of the industrial estate, and through an estate of new houses, which have been built on the site of the cattle market which operated alongside the railway. You will emerge into* **12** *Marlborough Road next to a bronze statue of a ram. Turn left, and the Town Hall, corn exchange and market square are on your right.*

Former GWR office building, now Historic England, with path leading to the tunnel.

9
THE RAILWAY ESTATE

THIS WALK BEGINS and ends at the cross-roads of pedestrianised streets at the heart of Swindon's shopping centre, attentively overseen by a benign golden lion on a plinth. His story can wait until we return. To the casual observer a less historical streetscape may be hard to imagine, but actually, lurking against a shopfront, small and unobtrusive, is one of the most significant clues to understanding Swindon's curious history. It is a milestone, enigmatically telling us the distance, 26 miles, to Semington, a village near Trowbridge in west Wiltshire.

Semington is where two canals joined, and the street is built over the course of one of them, the Wilts and Berks, which was completed in 1810, some three decades before the railway. The canal formed a kind of moat, defining the southern limit of the later railway town, and the points where it was bridged dictated the new settlement's street plan. Between, and parallel to, the canal and the railway ran a much older landscape feature, a road known as the Fleetway which connected towns to the west – Wootton Bassett and Malmesbury – with towns to the east – Faringdon and Oxford. We shall follow the course of the canal, then return by the old road (Faringdon Road) before exploring the railway village, the remains of the works, and the junction station.

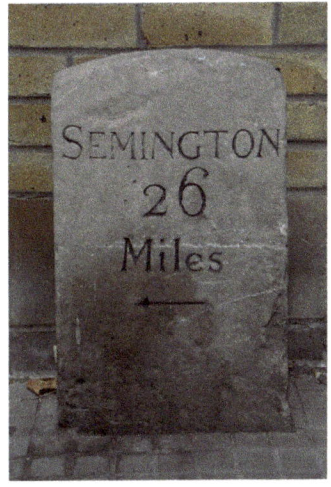

The canal milestone.

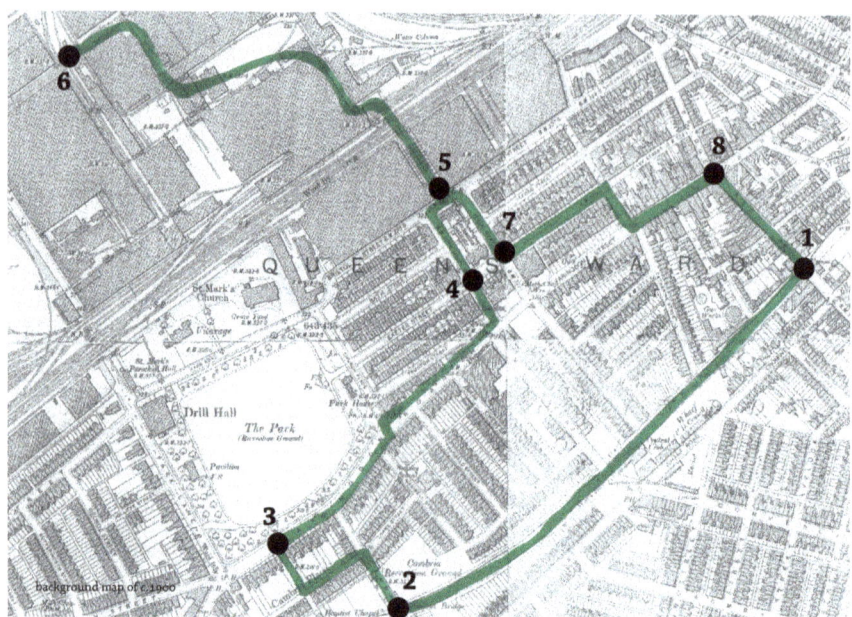

1 Set off from the milestone along Canal Walk, the shopping street between the Brunel plaza on the left and the Murray John Tower on the right, and continue in a straight line Do not be alarmed that your path takes you through and under a multi-storey car park, and under two road bridges. Continue until you reach the next bridge, Cambria Bridge, with its impressive display of mural street art.

When this portion of the canal was being built, in 1804, and for several decades afterwards, there was open countryside on both sides, with only a distant view of civilization in the shape of Old (or High) Swindon on the hill to the left and a few buildings at Even Swindon (the flat, low-lying end of the parish) to the right. From 1840 terraces of houses began to spread across the fields between the canal and the new railway tracks, slowly at first but rapidly after the 1860s, so that the landscape was transformed,

The line of the canal running beneath a car park.

THE RAILWAY ESTATE

Milton Road canal bridge.

and by the 1890s the canal's useful life was over. It had become irrelevant, and its course through Swindon was both an inconvenience and a health hazard. In 1914 the borough council purchased the Swindon portion and filled it in.

Everything now is late 20th century as we set off. But beyond the car park and road bridges is a world of private back gardens and Victorian brick. The smaller, earlier houses are to the right of the canal; to the left Curtis Street and its neighbours date from a building boom of the more affluent 1890s, by when the new town had long broken free from the canal's constraint, and these houses are consequently larger and better appointed.

2 *Do not walk under Cambria Bridge, but instead turn right into Cambria Bridge Road, and shortly left into Cambria Place. Halfway along, noting Cambria Baptist Chapel to the left, turn right and we emerge into Faringdon Road, opposite the former GWR Park.*

Our walk is now moving away from the canal to the world of the early railway settlement. In 1860-1 a rolling mill for iron rails was built at the works, and to construct and operate it workmen from south Wales were encouraged to move with their families to Swindon. At first they were accommodated in a former lodging-house known as the Barracks, which we shall encounter shortly, but by 1864 two rows of stone cottages, Cambria Place and Cambria Buildings (the south side of Faringdon Road), had been built for them. The project, which has been dubbed 'the second railway village', was perhaps financed by a block mortgage from a building society; at the heart of the community was the Welsh-speaking Baptist chapel, opened in 1866.

Mural beside Cambria Bridge.

When this Welsh colony was established private housing was already springing up further to the west along the ancient Fleetway, by then renamed Faringdon Road. Across the road in 1844 a field was given to the GWR by the lord of Eastcott manor in order to create a cricket ground and park, and this became the venue every August for a children's fete of gigantic proportions. The park was given by the GWR to the borough council in 1925, in exchange for land elsewhere which the company needed in order to extend the works. Beyond the park is visible the spire of St Mark's Church. This church was completed in 1845, and, despite standing aloof from most of its congregation, it became the centre of Anglican worship for the railway village and burgeoning new town.

Albion Street, off Cambria Bridge Road.

3 *Turn right and walk along the right hand side of Faringdon Road until you have crossed Maxwell Street. Use the pedestrian crossing to cross Faringdon Road, and continue along the left hand side. The terraces of stone cottages which make up the railway village are now on your left, and in due course you will arrive at the centrepiece of the village, Emlyn Square.*

The GWR Park, Faringdon Road, St Mark's Church in the distance.

Ignore if you can the tarmac and the traffic, and imagine where you are standing as an exercise in 1840s social engineering as significant in its way as the revolution in railway engineering occurring apace a few hundred metres away. Emlyn Square is a renaming of the fledgling town's high street, and ranged on either

THE RAILWAY ESTATE

The Railway Village Museum.

side are the roads and houses of a flawed new town. The deal was ingenious – in return for a lucrative catering contract at the station a developer would at its own expense build a town to house the company's workforce, then be free to take its rent. The flaw, as so often in such schemes, lay in the infrastructure – principally (in New Swindon's case) inadequate sanitation and drains. The new settlers, cutting-edge engineers and artisans, were unimpressed by their accommodation, but eagerly tackled other deficiencies themselves, by providing cultural, educational, medical and recreational facilities (most of which the far from benevolent company claimed as their own).

So here you will find, as I encourage you to walk around and explore, not only the rows of stone-built cottages, carefully restored and with their subtle idiosyncrasies of detail, but also the corner shops and pubs, the apartment block or barracks for single men (now The Platform, a music venue), the Turkish baths and swimming pool, the hospital and other medical services, and the centrepiece (now long dilapidated alas), the Mechanics Institute, which acted as library, theatre, lecture hall, and much else. You might also turn back to chapter 4, pages 79-90, where these buildings are described in more detail.

The Mechanics Institute, awaiting rescue from its dereliction.

Alley giving rear access to Railway Village terraces.

Such a townscape is not unique. It can be found at other railway creations – Crewe, Derby and Wolverton – and in more philanthropic and celebrated model towns fashioned by industrialists, such as Saltaire, Port Sunlight and Bournville; but here, in rural Victorian Wiltshire, the shock of the new must have been profound, and its survival for us to savour should be more appreciated and celebrated than it usually is.

4 *When you have finished immersing yourself in this alien Victorian world, walk to the far end of Emlyn Square, beyond the mechanics' institute, and you will find* **5** *the 'tunnel' entrance, which gave access from the village to the works, beneath the carriage manufactory and the railway lines. Walk through the tunnel and beyond it up the slope to the left, into what is now known as the Great Western Historic Area. Follow the signs across this area to the entrance of the Designer Outlet Village.*

The tunnel dates from the building of the carriage works in 1868 between the village and the original railway works buildings. In its heyday it was used by thousands of employees on their way to and from work. The impressive building at its northern end, which housed the GWR administration and drawing office, is now occupied by Historic England as its National Monuments Record Centre (see p. 162). As you make your way across this area you will encounter various buildings of the former railway works, and

The entrance to the tunnel.

some newcomers. These include Churchward House, the former works manager's office, with parallel railway tracks (known as a traversing table) in front of it. Next to this is STEAM, the Museum of the Great Western Railway. This is an essential destination, not only for those interested in railway locomotives and rolling stock, but also a mine of information about the social history of Swindon and of railway travel in general. Opposite is Heelis, the futuristic national headquarters of the National Trust, opened in 2005. And beyond is the entrance to the McArthurGlen Designer Outlet, which occupies

The traversing table.

former railway factory buildings, mostly dating from the great expansion of the 1870s, and incorporating the brass foundry, machine and boiler shops. Opened in 1997, it continuing success has made a major contribution to Swindon's efforts to regenerate and modernise.

6 *After the distraction of bargain hunting retrace your steps to the tunnel. When you emerge turn left and then right into Emlyn Square, walk along as far as* **7** *The Gluepot pub, then (after an optional refreshment stop) left along Reading Street. At the far end (East Street) turn right and then left into Fleet Street (pedestrianised). Continue as far as the cross-roads with* **8** *Bridge Street, turn right and walk back up to rejoin the golden lion where we began.*

Heelis, the National Trust headquarters.

East Street signals the end of the original railway village, and the beginning of Sheppard's Field. Its owner, John Henry Harding Sheppard, was a successful Old Town brewer who developed his field around 1870 to extend the layout, and gave each street one of his names. The terraces of cottages which covered his field have now, for the most part, been cleared away, apart from along the northern end, and the area has been redeveloped. In front of you large modern office blocks now fill the area between the railway station (away to your left) and the shopping centre (to your right).

Fleet Street.

On our short walk, via Fleet Street and Bridge Street, back to where we began, we encounter a great variety of building styles and dates. No-one would pretend that this is the most visually attractive Swindon streetscape, nor that its architecture is of great distinction, but it well illustrates the restlessness and continual modification to which the commercial heart of towns are subject. Fleet Street and Bridge Street were both built up with terraced housing during the 1850s, and the latter offered housewives in the formative years the means of escape across the canal to gather provisions from the Old Swindon shops away up on the hill. As Bridge Street, and its continuation

Bridge Street.

Regent Street, developed as the new town's shopping streets, most of the houses were adapted for retail use and later demolished, but a few survive above the shopfronts.

Next to the bridge, to which the street's name refers, was a canalside pub, the Golden Lion, which one entered beneath a magnificent stone lion over its doorway. The drawbridge, which could be raised when canal boats needed to pass beneath, was therefore always known as Golden Lion bridge, and the present statue is the reminder.

Golden Lion, Bridge Street.

Swindon Town Hall.

10
GROWING PAINS

TO BEGIN THIS WALK we must return to the sphinx-like golden lion, and reveal some more of his secrets. In the previous chapter we discovered the moat-like canal, and explored the railway town that developed behind it. Now we shall trace a second canal, and sample how New Swindon began to expand in all directions, despite the constraints that these older lines of communication imposed. But Swindon's extraordinary growth was dictated not only by topography – there were also economic factors (the ebb and flow of GWR fortunes), and a legal restraint, which placed lucrative development land out of bounds for years. Into this mix a third theme emerges, as the lava flow of Old Swindon running down its hill met the upstart terraces of New Swindon pushing up towards it. And finally the consummation, as old and new unite at the end of the Victorian century, and cement their union with a circus.

    A word of caution before we set off. Like all dynamic town centres Swindon has long been in a state of flux. Much has changed and is changing. So this walk will rapidly date, and it explores places that, though interesting to the topographer, are not the conventional haunts of sightseers and tourists.

    This is quite a long walk. But it can be split and walked in two sections, dividing at Regent Circus.

1 *Before setting off stand at the pedestrian cross-roads and take a look along The Parade, which is running east on the line of the former Wilts and Berks Canal, and notice* **2** *Fleming Way at the far end (in front of the Zurich office building). Now from the golden lion walk down Bridge Street (northwards)* and continue across Fleet Street, staying on Bridge Street until it ends opposite a station car park. Turn right along Station Road for a short distance and you will see across the road a **3** tunnel disappearing under the railway tracks. Explore the tunnel and then return to walk along Station Road until you arrive at the station forecourt.

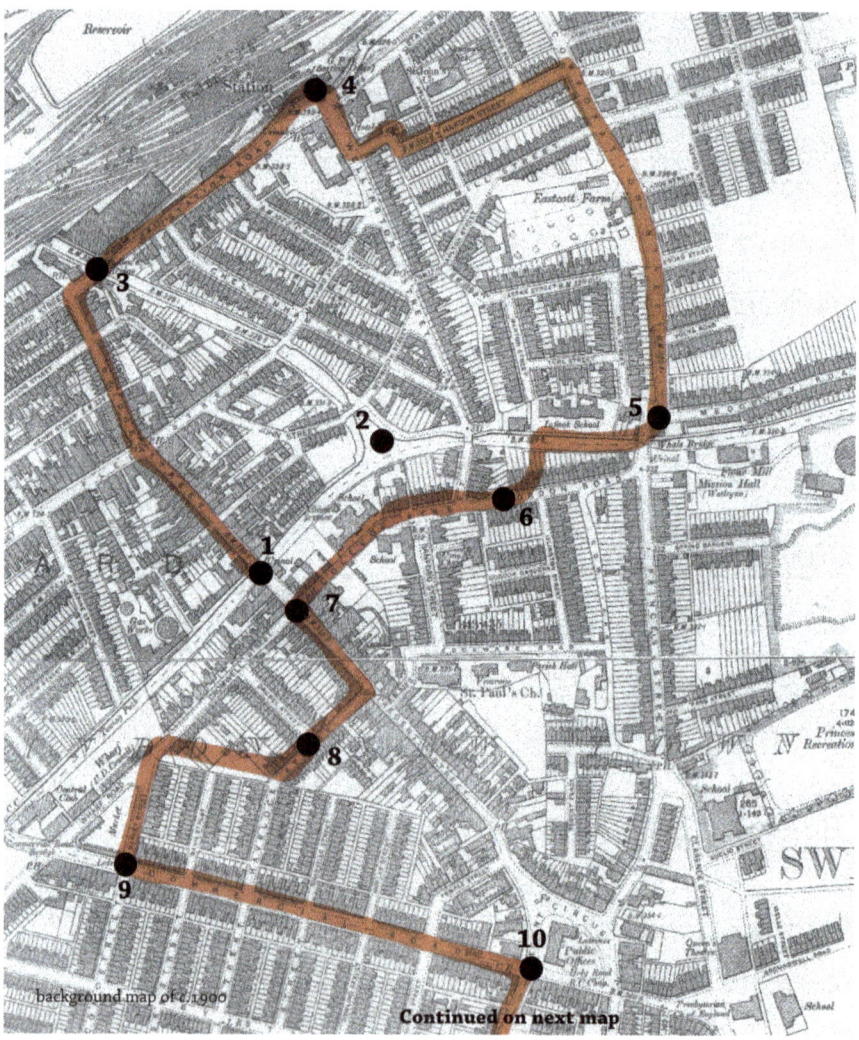

Bridge Street, as we discovered on the previous walk, was the route whereby the early settlers in New Swindon could cross the canal to reach the facilities of the older town on the hill. North of Fleet Street it deflects slightly, heading towards another constraining feature of the new town. This was a short second canal, the North Wilts, which branched from the Wilts and Berks just about where The Parade meets Fleming Way, and ran northwards for eight miles to Latton, to join another canal system, and thus to provide a link via the Thames with London, and via the Severn with the Midlands. Fleming Way is

The Fleming Way subway, a few days before it closed in 2023 as part of the redevelopment of the area. It occupied the approximate site of the junction of Swindon's two canals (no. 2 on map).

built on part of its course, and as we make our way through the tunnel it is not hard to see that we are following it. This canal was completed in 1819, some two decades before the railway was built above it, and there was a pub, the Union Tavern, and a bridge, Bullen's Bridge, next to the present car park entrance. Because it pre-dates the railway station and village, all the nearby roads followed the canal's diagonal course, and (although they have mostly been obliterated) the present confusing street pattern between the station and the town centre is an indirect result of the canal alignment. The canal was significant, too, in that it was one of the reasons why the GWR chose here to build its junction and works – stone could be transported along it for building and coal for

Railway bridge over the line of the North Wilts Canal.

fuelling. But of course, once the railways were built they led to the canal's demise.

Since 1972, when most of the Victorian era buildings were demolished, Swindon station has looked more like an

Swindon Station forecourt and offices.

office block (and currently disused) than a railway junction, although original buildings remain across the tracks, between platforms 2 and 3.

4 *Turn away from the station forecourt and walk down Wellington Street a short way, then first left into Haydon Street (unmarked at first), and at its far end right into Corporation Street. Continue past the Carfax roundabout to the* **5** *Whalebridge junction, noting the large mural painting and the terrace of houses, Medgbury Street, on the end wall of which it is painted.*

When the railway station was conceived and built, and for several decades afterwards, most passengers did not begin or end their journeys at Swindon. And if they did, they would not have headed off down Wellington Street towards town, as we have done, because there was no town and no street here, only an increasingly obsolete canal. Not until the 1870s, when the fields of Lower Eastcott Farm began to be built over with terraces of houses such as Haydon Street, was there any reason to come here. Corporation Street was merely a track leading to the farm (which stood opposite where Lagos Street begins now) until the 1890s.

Its name, which cannot be older than 1900 when Swindon Corporation came into being, refers to the corporation's electricity works and tram depot; these were built on the site of the farm in 1903 and 1906 respectively. The incongruous name, Carfax, for the roundabout here derives from the activities of one of the several small building societies which erected houses in the area – this one was from Oxford, and the terraced streets all bore Oxford-sounding names, Merton, Turl, Oriel, Carfax. They disappeared under a car stack, which itself disappeared in 2015. Beyond is the major intersection, Whalebridge, which takes its name from a whale-shaped bridge which crossed the canal here. Beneath where the dual carriageway is now ran the canal and alongside it was a terrace of cottages, Cetus Buildings (*cetus* is Latin for whale). But the canal is not forgotten. On the end wall of the later terrace is Ken White's mural of another canal bridge, our old friend the Golden Lion. The man in the foreground is Swindon poet Alfred Williams – a certain I.K. Brunel lurks at the back. Commonplace now, murals such as this were practically unheard of when he first painted it in 1976, and Ken has gone on to international celebrity, working on hundreds of street-art projects across Europe and North America, including other murals in Swindon.

The mural at Whalebridge (but depicting Golden Lion bridge).

5 *Cross this major road junction, Fleming Way, heading diagonally to the right, to take the minor road between the health centre and a large hotel, and then right into* **6** *College Street, which runs beneath an overhead car stack. Follow this around until it meets* **7** *Regent Street. Turn left, and then right along the south side of the Brunel shopping centre until you arrive at the Brunel statue in Havelock Square.*

In 2023, as this book is prepared for publication, Fleming Way is undergoing major transformation, not expected to be complete until 2025. The name has nothing to do with penicillin, nor James Bond; Harold Fleming was a footballer, a local legend who played for Swindon Town and England, and died in 1955. The construction of Fleming Way along the line of the old canal was an attempt to keep cars and shoppers apart, very much in vogue among town planners in the 1960s. The shopping streets were pedestrianised and the cars were diverted along this elevated road into multi-storey car parks. Now the tables are

Plaque commemorating the GWR School.

turned, and Fleming Way is to become a 'boulevard' for walkers, cyclists and public transport, with cars forbidden. The area is being revitalised, and one of the first results is the NHS health centre, opened in 2017. College Street takes us straight back 150 years, as its name derives from the GWR School built here after legislation in 1870 made school provision for all children compulsory. That school was demolished in 1961 – Tesco took its place, and there is a plaque commemorating it on the walkway down to The Parade. But a second school was built in 1881 nearby, in Sanford Street, and this imposing building remains, though

Sanford Street Boys School.

Regent Street, with the Brunel Centre on the left.

no longer a school. Facing us as we emerge into Regent Street is the Brunel Centre, which replaced streets of small houses with a shopping mall during the early 1970s – notice that the earlier Marks and Spencer façade has been retained (the store's closure was announced in 2023). Around the corner a statue of Brunel himself (a copy of one on the Victoria Embankment in London) presides over the centre's entrance.

8 *Take a look along Havelock Street, noticing the change of alignment, but then continue around the edge of the Brunel centre and beneath the spiral service road until you reach a paved open space with several large trees. Turn left (Market Street) with the tent-like indoor market (currently, in 2023, closed) on your right and walk up to* **9** *Commercial Road,*

Brunel statue.

noticing that a residential road continues straight across and up the hill to a grassed area. This is Radnor Street Cemetery which we shall visit shortly. Walk up Commercial Road, noticing the variety of older and newer commercial buildings, and the residential side roads, until you reach the Town Hall on your left. **10** This is Regent Circus, which we shall explore presently. Meanwhile turn right up Eastcott Hill.

Havelock Street looking up to Commercial Road.

Nearly everywhere this walk takes us to from now until we reach the top of the hill was built during the late 1880s and 1890s. Swindon around 1880 was bursting at the seams, but the fields surrounding it were out of bounds because their owner was bankrupt and most of his land, the Rollestone estate, was held in Chancery until 1885 or later. If you stand in the square, looking along Havelock Street, you are facing the explosion of housebuilding that followed as soon as it became available. The centrepiece of the new development was a main shopping street, Commercial Road, which would form the spine of a grid of terraced residential streets aligned on it. The older Regent Street, which it was intended (but failed) to supplant, was set on a different alignment, so that where you are standing marks the awkward junction of competing town plans, a kind of geological fault, as we described it earlier (pp.105-7 with maps).

The 'tipsy tent' market with Murray John Tower beyond.

With all this in mind our walk along Commercial Road begins to make sense. But before that we encounter the 'tipsy tent' market (standing closed in 2023) which was built in 1995 on the site of an open, and then covered, market which formed part of the Commercial Road masterplan, and which was demolished in 1977. The commercial hub at one end, then, a long straight shopping street, and then the administrative hub, the Town Hall, at the other. But before we explore Regent Circus we should immerse ourselves in the terraced streets which typify *fin de siècle* Swindon.

After turning up Eastcott Street you will soon encounter Crombey Street, so cross with care and take the next right, **11** *Dixon Street, and walk its full length, to the entrance to Radnor Street Cemetery. When you have explored this urban wildlife oasis leave by the top entrance (Kent Road).*

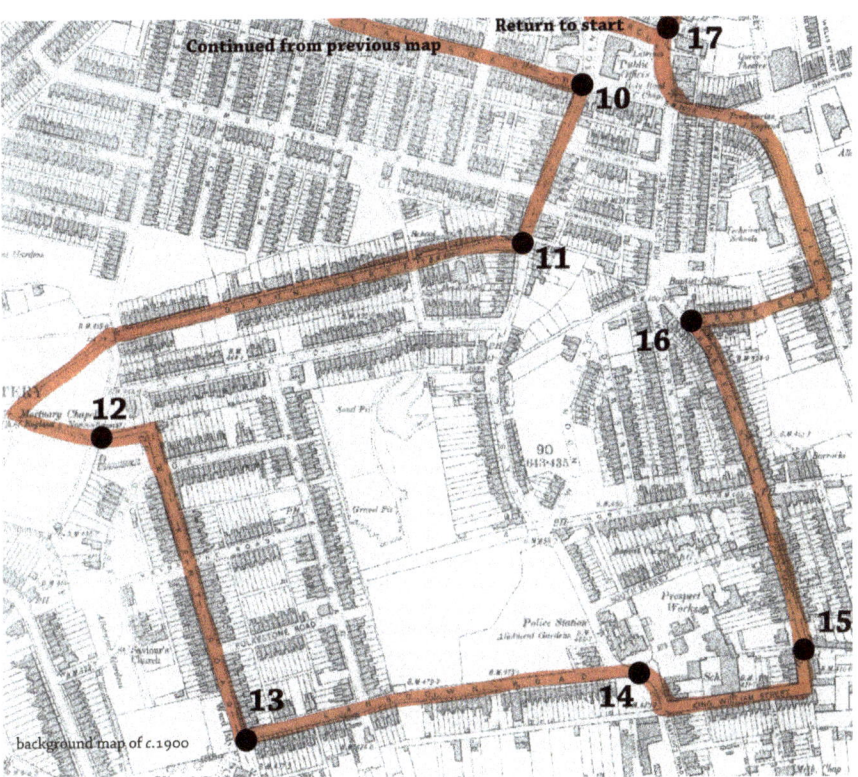

Dixon Street.

Dixon Street, one of the more varied and interesting of these late Victorian streets, was built progressively along the escarpment known then as Gilbert's Hill, overlooking the town, during the 1880s and 1890s. Its infants' and girls' school, signed and dated by its architect, Brightwen Binyon, arrived early, in 1880, and was soon joined by the chapel opposite, built by Presbyterians in 1885 but used by a minority but very ancient sect, the Moravians, from 1899. It may seem a slog up the hill, but the reward is a saunter around Swindon's secret lung, a nature reserve and wildlife haven since 2005, and a fitting resting place for the town's pioneers and unsung heroes and heroines, the Radnor Street Cemetery. Laid out in 1880, some 33,000 Swindonians had been buried here before it closed in 1970. When conceived it lay near the frontier between Old and New Swindon, two separate local authorities, who co-operated and jointly funded it for the benefit of both communities – an early sign of their inevitable coalescence, as Swindon Borough, twenty years later.

Grave of Mayor Lapper Morse.

The Dixon Street entrance to Radnor Street Cemetery.

12 *Turn right along Kent Road and walk up as far as* **13** *Lansdown Road (4th on left). Turn left and walk to its end. Lansdown Road has an interesting variety of terraces, and a quite grand 1869 block near its end with ornamental heads. Turn right into* **14** *Eastcott Hill and immediately left (King William Street).*

Why, you may ask, have I brought you to these apparently nondescript terraces, and why are they all named after towns in Kent – Ashford, Maidstone, Folkestone, Hythe? Well, precisely because they typify so much of Swindon's adolescence, from the 1860s to about 1920, built up piecemeal by small-scale entrepreneurs. John Harding Sheppard, son of an Old Town brewer (who named several earlier streets after himself), inherited this land, sold it for development, and went to live in Kent, where his brother William practised medicine (in Ashford).

Diana Dors birthplace plaque.

Notice, incidentally, as we stroll up Kent Street, the blue plaque above Nos. 61-2, placed here in 2017, which records the birthplace in 1931 of Diana Dors, film actress and glamour icon. But how could she be born in both houses – the simple answer is that at the time they both formed part of a nursing home?

As we turn into Lansdown Road we have entered a slightly different milieu from either Sheppard or Dors. This street is earlier (recorded in 1869) and belongs to Old Swindon, not New. And as we progress we can see that the housing styles become more varied. On the left side most are from the early 20th century, on the right are older short terraces, a former bottle factory, and at the far end a grander house with plaster faces staring out at passers-by. Eastcott Hill strikes a discordant note, its derelict bus garage abandoned in 2016, although in fact the line of the winding road is far older – medieval perhaps – than any of the residential roads around it. In King William Street we return to the 1870s.

Walk along King William Street and turn left at the end into **15** *Prospect Place and then Prospect Hill, Shortly before the Beehive pub turn right into* **16** *Cross Street which leads into Victoria Road. Turn left and continue back down to Regent Circus.*

King William Street School, the former National School for Old Town.

Just as the tide of New Swindon rose little by little further up the hill, so the lava of Old Swindon began to flow down to meet it. We pass the Old Town National School built here in 1871, and enlarged in 1890, to replace an older church school which the population had outgrown. Notice at the corner a former drill hall and armoury, used to train voluntary army reservists in the years leading up to the first world war, then turn down Prospect Place and Hill, the older link between the two towns before Victoria Road was built. Here are chapels, a pub, and a pleasant mix of building styles, stone, brick and render, including a terrace masquerading as almshouses, with just a glimpse of the eponymous prospect over the upper Thames to the Cotswolds as we descend. To our left South Street followed by North Street tell us by their names that we are still in Old Swindon, but before we reach Cross Street (named perhaps after the Home Secretary of the 1870s, Richard Cross) and the Beehive pub we have definitely returned to New Swindon. Crossing to Victoria Road we encounter a proud statement of late-Victorian industry and self-improvement, the redbrick Technical Institution building of 1897 (forerunner of Swindon College).

Cottages on Prospect Hill.

This northern stretch of Victoria Road was begun during the 1870s, to link the Old and New Towns, and was at first unimaginatively named

New Road. But it was not until 1888 that it was properly made up, and then cottages and larger houses began to spring up alongside, including Buscott Terrace (now Indian restaurants and shops), which faces us across the road as we turn the corner. And so we arrive at Regent Circus.

Stroll around Regent Circus, Princes Street and **17** *Theatre Square. Then make your way back down Regent Street until you come to the crossing of pedestrian streets, presided over by the golden lion, where our walk began.*

The grand name sounds as if it has been imported from London, and indeed there was a Regent Circus partly built between 1811 and 1822 next to London's Regent's Park, but never completed or so-named. Back in Swindon a farmstead and hamlet, Upper Eastcott, had existed long before the railway town was thought of, at the southern end of what became Swindon's Regent Street, roughly where Theatre Square and Princes Street are now. It was here that 'Old Charlie', the Yorkshireman we encountered in chapter 5, speculated with his terrace of cottages, York Place. As part of the Commercial Road and Victoria Road development the New Town Board decided that it would build its new headquarters, the Town Hall, here, opposite York Place, and so the area was laid out. Its name, at first, was to be Trafalgar Square, then on second thoughts (too posh), York Square, and eventually, by 1899, Regent Circus.

The Town Hall was built quite rapidly in 1890-1, designed by Ipswich architect Brightwen Binyon, who had earlier been responsible for a number of Swindon's schools. With its 90-foot high clock tower, it remains one of Swindon's most iconic buildings, now sympathetically

The last survivor of the original York Square (Regent Circus) development: a solicitor's office dated 1891.

Regent Circus cinema and restaurant complex, completed in 2015.

complemented by the adjoining Central Library of 2008. Most of the other buildings around Regent Circus are fairly modern, notably the Wyvern Theatre of 1971 and the cinema, restaurant and (closed) superstore complex of 2015 on the site of the former Swindon College. MECA (Music Entertainment Cultural Arena), the enormous shed-like structure facing Princes Street, is the former art-deco Regent Cinema built in 1929. To imagine Regent Circus in its Edwardian heyday take a look at the façade of Bevir's solicitor's office (no. 36) facing the front of the Town Hall.

From Regent Circus it is a short stroll down the shop-lined Regent Street. Notice that many of the shops occupy quite small premises, as they are the successors to the cottages and private houses that sprang up along it during the 1850s and 1860s. Gradually they were converted to small and fairly insignificant shops, which led to the sarcastic name, Regent Street. When I first knew the street, in the 1970s, the roofs of Victorian houses still poked above many of the shopfronts, but over time they seem all to have been rebuilt or disguised.

11
TRAVELS THROUGH SUBURBIA

SWINDON IN 1900, when its population was around 50,000, was small enough to explore on foot, and the three walks offered in chapters 8-10 have taken us, more or less, to the limits of the Victorian and Edwardian town. But if we are to decode modern Swindon we must explore also its suburbs, an area so vast that it is scarcely possible to contemplate walking it all – not, at any rate, within the compass of a book such as this. Instead I suggest that the suburban explorer uses Swindon's buses. Currently (2023) a 'Dayrider' ticket costs less than £5 and allows unlimited travel all day throughout the built-up area, on routes which, typically, run at 15-30 minute frequency. This chapter explains how, and to some extent why, Swindon's suburbs have developed as they have, and then suggests bus routes you might take in order to see for yourselves.

In principle, anyone who journeys from a historic town centre to its outermost suburbs will be a time traveller, moving from the distant past to the present day, because layers of suburbs tend to be added around the town's periphery one after another. Such a journey will be erratic, of course, because other factors – natural obstacles, landownership, previous land use and existing settlements – will have affected and impeded the town's growth; but in general terms it will serve as a model. And in Swindon's case (and the same could be demonstrated elsewhere) another factor is at play. For most of its recent history growth has been, one might say, centripetal. Its suburbs looked to the centre, for employment (principally the railway works), commerce, retail and leisure. Suburban dwellers came into town for everything they needed.

That is not the case now. If anything Swindon has become centrifugal (the opposite of centripetal); working, shopping, socialising now take place around the periphery, in West Swindon, North Swindon, Wichelstow and more still to come. And much of what used to happen in the centre has been sucked out to these satellite communities, substantial towns in all but name. To take an example, Swindon's largest employer currently is Nationwide Building Society, with headquarters in Pipers Way on the south-eastern fringe of Old Town. East Wichel, a residential suburb of the 21st century, with its own shops and other facilities, is scarcely a kilometre away, so the two could, and to some extent probably do, function symbiotically without any reference to the rest of Swindon.

That is one consideration. Another is the changing fashion of residential suburban development. Even Swindon, Gorse Hill and parts of Rodbourne were laid out either side of 1900 as rectilinear grids of terraced housing. Pinehurst in the 1920s followed the garden city ideal pioneered in Letchworth and Welwyn. In Moredon, Gorse Hill and along Marlborough Road beyond Old Town we can see typical 1930s ribbon development

of semi-detached bay-windowed houses along avenues and main roads. Then came the 1950s and 1960s London overspill housing of Park, Walcot and Stratton, and local authority estates at Moredon, Cheney Manor and Penhill, including at the latter high-rise blocks of flats. By the 1970s the focus had moved to more spacious, car-owning suburban dwellers, on estates at Covingham, Eldene and Liden to the east, and Haydon Wick to the north. Gradually the idea of separating roads from people, introducing cycle paths, walkways and abundant green space, took root, so that West Swindon, from the 1970s and 1980s, became Wiltshire's Milton Keynes. North Swindon followed in the 1990s, but by then the vogue was for faux-

This view of Swindon from the south illustrates a sequence of suburban development. Beginning in the foreground, rural Wroughton's farmland has been crossed by the M4 motorway, which exercises a barrier to Swindon's southern expansion. Just beyond are the very recent Wichel estates, and then a green strip (the low-lying meadowland of the River Ray. The ground rises to the Okus ridge on which Old Town was built, and where modern houses (in front of the Murray John Tower from our viewpoint) have replaced the former Princess Margaret Hospital. Victorian New Swindon lies beyond, largely concealed apart from its roofs and the Murray John Tower. Behind is the well wooded ridge on which the North Swindon estates have encroached towards Blunsdon, and in the far distance the Cotswold Hills form the horizon.

traditional houses of incongruous variety, after the Poundbury model. And this has continued at Wichelstowe, like Poundbury a community entirely detached from its parent.

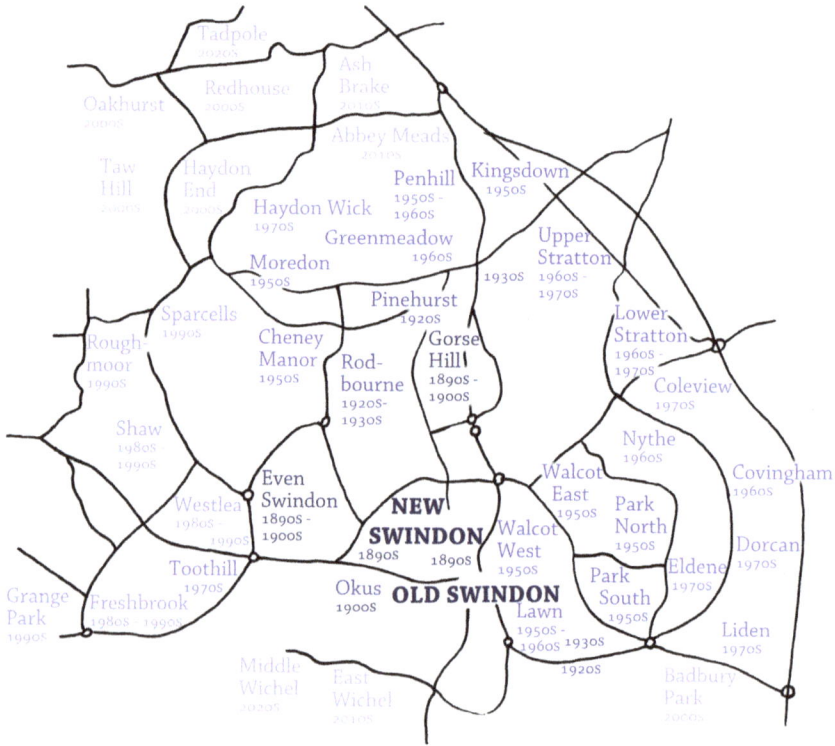

Maps describe the sequence of development better than words. Armed with the map provided here, and the ideas I have tried to instil, you should be able to make sense of the view from the window of any Swindon bus. But to help you here are a few suggestions.

Our first excursion leads us through some of the older suburbs, and takes us nowhere more recent than the 1960s, when Swindon was still primarily focused on the railway works, but was also witnessing rapid expansion, as London overspill brought new people and new industries. Buses (currently route 17) steer a roughly north-south course between Penhill and Park South. Leaving the centre by County Road and beneath the railway tracks the Penhill bus plies along Cricklade Road, the high street of one of Swindon's earliest suburbs, Gorse Hill.

St Barnabas church was begun here in 1884, and residential streets appeared soon after. The older terraced houses along Cricklade Road have been converted to small shops, but as we progress towards the Moonrakers junction most are larger and later, of the 1930s, and remain residential. The loop of Penhill Drive was laid out in the early 1950s, and built up over the next decade with council housing ranged – as was then fashionable – in terraced blocks away from traffic, and dominated by three high-rise blocks of flats.

1950s high-rise and low-rise on the Park London overspill estate.

Returning to the centre our bus then takes us along Groundwell Road, a largely Edwardian development, with gridded streets to its north, and into Walcot along Upham Road; this is somewhat later, laid out in the late 1920s, although most housing in Walcot is post-war. We negotiate the major artery, Queen's Drive of 1955, which is a very significant boundary between pre-war and post-war Swindon, and private and public housing, and our bus makes its way around Park South, one of the products of the 1950s London overspill, with more high-rise flats and its centrepiece shopping mall, Cavendish Square, and then returns to the town centre.

Our next venture will be to the North Swindon Orbital Retail Park (route 5), which introduces us on its way along Rodbourne Road to two other early suburbs, Even Swindon (built up in rectilinear fashion during the 1880s and 1890s), and Rodbourne, where the houses are a little later, early 20th century, with further development in the 1920s and 1930s. The ancient settlement of Rodbourne Cheney lay outside Swindon borough until 1928, but was becoming suburban, and in 1929, once boundaries were altered to include it within Swindon, older road names were consolidated into Cheney Manor Road in 1929. Rodbourne

included a second ancient settlement, Moredon, so after our bus has passed the medieval church, it follows the old roads of Moredon village (Moredon Road and The Street), now completely suburbanised, to reach Haydon. This too had medieval origins, but

Rodbourne Cheney, with its medieval parish church, became completely suburbanised during the 1920s and 1930s, but the process had begun somewhat earlier, as these Edwardian houses near the church testify.

what we see dates from a massive expansion during the 1970s, and a second wave, which created North Swindon from about 2000, with its Orbital Retail Park around a supermarket of staggering size and an even larger car park.

There is more to see if we switch here to a bus for Taw Hill (route 11), which drives us ever further through newer suburbs, Redhouse and Oakhurst, largely embracing the millennial fad for incongruous juxtapositions of various architectural styles from the past. Our bus returns us to the Orbital Park, and if we

The Orbital Retail Park, North Swindon.

stick with it we will travel back through the decades – Haydon Wick of the 1970s, Greenmeadow of the 1960s, and then Pinehurst, which was Swindon's 1920s attempt to provide homes for heroes after World War One by creating a garden city. And so back to the centre. But there is more the bus will show us. Sit tight and it will take us up the hill to the streets of Old Town, where Swindon began, and then to the beginning of Marlborough Road. The houses here are larger than most that we have seen, with bay windows, and typical of inter-war ribbon development. At the roundabout we turn into Pipers Way, built in the 1970s to serve a large commercial and industrial complex (headquarters of an oil company), which has now been replaced by modern flats. Past the Nationwide campus we cross the main road south from Swindon and return to the 21st century, though with 11th-century nomenclature. Wichel may have farmed and lived in a cottage here before the Normans invaded; and he has given his name to one of Swindon's newest and most imaginative suburban centres – in 2023 still a work in progress, but complete with a restored stretch of the Wilts and Berks Canal, flanked by a supermarket, gym, and restaurant.

Having returned to central Swindon one further bus journey (routes 1, 1A or 1B) will allow us to sample West Swindon, the major residential, commercial and industrial expansion that began in the 1970s at Toothill, soon after the M4 had opened throughout with a junction nearby, and continued into the 1990s, extending as far as the gates of Lydiard Park. Our bus will take us around and along a bewildering maze of roundabouts and leafy lanes, past cycle paths, open spaces, walkways and culs-de-sac, and calling in at the neighbourhood centre, with supermarket, gym and library.

Characteristic of West Swindon are trees, open grassland, footpaths and public art.

For those wishing to exploit their day bus-pass to the maximum there are other horizons to explore – Covingham and Liden to the east, Blunsdon to the north, Badbury Park and the Great Western Hospital campus to the south-east, Okus to the south-west. And as Swindon continues to grow new routes will be introduced and old routes will change. At the end of the day any attempt to pin Swindon down and decipher it will fail – it continues to grow and change, at the edges and at the centre. Long may it do so!

Great Western Hospital.

DELVING DEEPER

A SHORT BOOK such as this cannot do justice to a subject as large as Swindon. Whole areas of great interest have been entirely omitted, or merely mentioned in passing. But if this book has succeeded in its aim of fuelling your interest in local history, there are several things which you could do next to unravel more of the Swindon code.

A good starting point would be to visit museums. As I write (October 2023) the displays and exhibits are being prepared for Swindon Museum in its new home within the council offices in Euclid Street, planned to open in 2024. This will include works from Swindon's outstanding collection of 20th-century British art, too long hidden from view. STEAM, the Great Western Railway Museum, is not just for railway buffs; its displays include a great deal about Swindon and its importance in railway history. The Railway Village Museum, managed by the Mechanics Institution Trust, is open occasionally, and details are posted on their website. Lydiard House Museum, within Lydiard Park, has been owned by Swindon since 1943 and is currently open Wednesdays to Sundays. Also owned by Swindon, and run by a trust, is the Richard Jefferies Museum, the farmhouse at Coate where he was born. Not a museum exactly, but Radnor Street Cemetery has a group of friends who lead walks around it describing the lives of ordinary and extraordinary Swindonians buried there. Two major national collections are also based in Swindon. The Historic England Archives (previously the National Monuments Record) is housed in the former GWR headquarters building, and is available to researchers. The National Collections Centre of the Science Museum is being developed on the former RAF Wroughton airfield site just south of Swindon, and plans to be open from 2024.

Although both these collections have libraries, the principal collection of books, periodical literature, and other printed material relating to the Swindon area is housed in the local studies section on the second floor of Swindon Central Library. With its helpful and knowledgeable professional staff this is the starting place for anyone researching Swindon's history. They also administer the Swindon and District History Network, which brings together interested societies and individuals for regular meetings. Most archives relating to Swindon are held not there, but at the Wiltshire and Swindon History Centre in Chippenham, staffed by equally helpful professionals.

It goes without saying that all these organisations have websites or a web presence (such as Facebook and blogs), and these can be used to find out more, including opening times. A great many sources of value to local history research are now available online, and anyone embarking on a local study should explore the National Archives research guides and the publications and online events of the British Association for Local History.

A book of this nature, intended merely as an introduction to a town's history, cannot be encumbered with extensive notes and references, although it is the product of wide reading, research and fieldwork over many years, and is heavily indebted to the work of others, past and present. Described below are the most important published books about the history of Swindon that I have used, with comments about what they cover.

The archaeology and early history of the Swindon area have been comprehensively covered by Bernard Phillips, *The Archaeology of the Borough of Swindon* (Hobnob Press, 2021).

Most aspects of the history of Swindon are summarised and fully referenced in the authoritative treatment by Elizabeth Crittall and others in *Victoria History of Wiltshire*, vol.9, (1970). Because it is now more than 50 years old this does not cover Swindon's recent history, and it is restricted to the ancient parish of Swindon, so does not cover parts of the town formerly in Rodbourne Cheney or Stratton St Margaret.

DELVING DEEPER

The fullest account of the development of the railway works and village, and of its buildings, is by John Cattell and Keith Falconer, *Swindon: the legacy of a railway town*, (HMSO, 1995).

Two compendia of useful information about very many aspects of Swindon's history and popular culture, derived in part from a card index once maintained in the reference library, are by Mark Child, *The Swindon Book* (Hobnob Press, 2013) and *The Swindon Book Companion* (Hobnob Press, 2015). Mark also wrote *Swindon: an Illustrated History* (Breedon Books, 2002).

There have been three major studies of Swindon from a sociological point of view at different periods in its expansion. The first was by Kenneth Hudson, *An Awkward Size for a Town: a study of Swindon at the 100,000 mark* (David & Charles, 1967). This was followed by Michael Harloe, *Swindon: a town in transition* (Heinemann, 1975), and then by Martin Boddy and others, *City for the 21st Century: globalisation, planning and urban change* (Policy Press, 1997).

The key planning document which played a major influence on the town's development was *Swindon: a Study for Further Expansion* (Swindon Borough Council, 1968), known from its cover as the 'Silver Book'.

Older substantial histories of Swindon are by William Morris, *Swindon: Reminiscences, Notes and Relics of ye Old Wiltshire Towne* (Swindon Advertiser, 1885, reprinted Tabard Press, 1970); Frederick Large, *A Swindon Retrospect, 1855-1930* (Borough Press, 1932, reprinted Redbrick Publishing, 1984); and L V Grinsell and others, *Studies in the History of Swindon* (Swindon Borough Council, 1950). This last volume includes material written in preparation for the *Victoria History* article, as well as John Betjeman's essay on architecture.

The principal journal for papers about Wiltshire's history, including Swindon, has since 1854 been the *Wiltshire Archaeological and Natural History Magazine* (116 volumes and in progress). Since 1939 the Wiltshire Record Society and its predecessor have published editions of historical records, including many relevant to Swindon (75 volumes and in progress).

Very many books have been written about Swindon railway works and its manufactures, principally for the enthusiast. And there are numerous well-researched studies of specific aspects of the town's history, including its churches, pubs, war record, football team, street names, theatre, and many other topics; also histories of specific areas, biographies of Swindonians and collections of old photographs. Swindon Central Library's local studies collection is the obvious place to explore this cornucopia.

For those interested in West Swindon a history uniform with this one is being published around the same time, by Angela Atkinson, Frances Bevan and Roger Ogle, *West Swindon: what the eye doesn't see* (Hobnob Press, 2023).

ACKNOWLEDGEMENTS

My first debt is to Roger Trayhurn, now retired, under whom I was initiated into librarianship – and Swindon– and who served as the town's reference librarian for half a century. I owe a great deal also to Darryl Moody, his successor, and to his colleagues Jenny Ackrill and Sara Steel, who run what must be one of the best local studies library services anywhere. My third enormous debt is to my friends the staff of Wiltshire and Swindon History Centre in Chippenham, but for whom any research into Wiltshire's history would be virtually impossible. It is my pleasure also to thank my editor, Louise Ryland-Epton, for her enthusiasm for this project and her support.

My formal thanks are due to the following for permission to reproduce material in their ownership or care: Kirsty Phillips (daughter of the late Bernard Phillips); National Library of New Zealand; Roger Ogle; Swindon Borough Council; Wiltshire Archaeological and Natural History Society; Wiltshire and Swindon History Centre. I thank also the Mechanics Institution Trust for giving me access to, and allowing me to photograph, rooms inside the Railway Village Museum.

Except where otherwise stated I took all the modern photographs between 2020 and 2023.

NOTE that in captions abbreviations used include WANHS for Wiltshire Archaeological and Natural History Society; WSA for Wiltshire and Swindon Archives; and WSHC for Wiltshire and Swindon History Centre (the repository for WSA). Wilts Museum at Devizes is owned by WANHS.

INDEX

This is an index of names and places. A few terms, which appear on almost every page, have not been indexed. These include Great Western Railway, GWR, (Railway) Works, and Swindon.

Abbey Meads 20, 140
Albert Street 93, 157
Allied Dunbar 132
Amis, Mark 143
Anderson, Alexander 156
Anderson Almshouses 156
Andover 115
Apsley House 61, 157–9
Arclite 124, 132
Armstrong, Vickers 122
ASDA 138
Ashford Road 101, 183
Ashton Keynes 15
Aubrey, John 7, 39–40, 42–3, 52–3
Avon, River (Bristol) 52–3

Badbury 22
Badbury Park 194
Badbury villa 19, 21
Badbury Wick 26
Barbury 13
Barclays Bank, High Street 154
Barnstaple 84
Barracks, The 89–90, 104, 144, 165, 167
Bath 32, 57, 62, 65, 67, 80, 84, 93, 143, 150, 155, 158
Bath Road 61, 109, 157–9
Bath Street 79
Bath Terrace 158
Bayeux 26
BBC Wiltshire 158

Bedfordshire 101
Beehive pub 184
Bell Inn 47, 154
Berkshire 33
Bertram, T.H. 74
Betjeman, John 47, 60, 86, 99, 109, 111, 120, 155–6, 197
Bevir's office 186
Binyon, Brightwen 182, 185
Birmingham 63, 68, 79
Blackford family 155
Blacksmith's Street 47, 155
blacksmith's 47, 155
Blagrove 23
Blunsdon (St Andrew) 11, 20, 23–4, 26, 29, 142, 189, 194
Bournville 168
Bowling Green Lane 160
Bowly, brewer 154
Box Tunnel 62, 64, 79
Bradan Weg 22
Braydon Forest 11, 47
Bristol 52–3, 62, 64–5, 67, 73–4, 79, 98, 116
Bristol Street 79, 97
Britannia Place 38, 61, 93
British Railways 119
Britton, John 32–3, 50, 52, 59
Broad Street 107–8, 125
Broadway, The 22
Brock Hill 45, 155, 157

INDEX

Brookwell Hill 45–6
Broome 13, 28, 42
Broome Manor 34
Brunel, Isambard K 52, 62, 64, 66, 68, 71, 74, 82–3, 102, 113, 177, 179
Brunel Centre 104, 135, 179
Brunel Plaza 106, 134, 164
Buchanan, Sir Colin 128
Buckinghamshire 79
Buckworth 156
Bull Street 48
Bullen's Bridge 175
Burderop Down 13
Burgeys, Elye 39
Buscott Terrace 185
Butterworth, Rose and Morrison 101

Cambria Bridge 59, 104, 164–5
Cambria Baptist Chapel 104, 165
Cambria Place 104, 165–6
Canal Walk 59, 164
Carfax roundabout 176–7
Carfax Street 101, 177
Cavendish Square 191
Ceatta's hill 23
Cennick, John 50
Cetus Buildings 102–3, 177
Chaddington 23, 53
Charles I, king 40
'Charlie, Old' 100, 102, 185
Cheltenham 62, 64–5, 68, 93, 115, 155, 161
Cheltenham and Gloucester Building Society 136
Cheltenham Street 101
Cheshire 79
Chippenham 67
'Chipping Swindon' 38
Chiseldon 13, 19, 23, 26, 124
Christ Church 94, 110, 152, 154–7, 189
Church Well 151
Churchward, G.J. 117–18, 121
Churchward House 76, 169
Cirencester 17, 43, 62, 143
Cleveland Farm 15
Coate 34, 109–10, 143, 195
Coate Water (Reservoir) 56, 141

Cobbett, William 61
Cobden Road 101
College Street 177–8
Collett, C.B. 118
Commonhead roundabout 17
Compton's factory 98
Congregational Chapel, Newport Street 51
Corallian limestone ridge 11, 13, 23–4
County Ground 115
County Road 54, 190
Covingham 17, 127, 189, 194
Cowley, Oxford 122
Cranfield University 143
Crewe 71, 79, 168
Cricklade 13, 21, 44, 54, 65, 127, 141, 145
Cricklade Road 190–1
Cricklade Street 45–7, 152, 155,
Croft Road 160
Crombey Street 181
Cross Street 184
Crown Inn 154
Curtis Street 165

Dammas Lane 34, 150
Dauntsey Vale 53
Dean, Forest 57
Derby 168
Devizes 10, 53
Devizes Road 38, 49, 61, 158
Devon 6
Dewell Mews 161
Didcot 64
Dixon Street 4, 112, 181–2
Dolyn, Constance 39
Domesday Book 23–6, 37
Dorcan 17, 21, 127
Dorcan brook 17
Dors, Diana 140, 183
Dorset 13, 93, 155
Dublin 82
Dunbar, Allied 132
Dundee 78
Dunsford, William 57, 61
Durocornovium 17–19, 21, 33–5

East Street 169–70
East Swindon 28
East Wichelstow 188
Eastbury Way 141
Eastcott 24, 26, 28–9, 42–3, 47, 54, 64, 166
Eastcott Farm 59
Eastcott Hill 91, 99, 103, 109, 157, 180, 183
Eastcott House 154
Eastcott, Lower (Farm) 176
Eastcott Street 181
Eastcott, Upper (Farm) 58, 100, 103, 185
Eastern Villages 145
Edward III, king 39
Elcombe 11
Eldene 26, 127, 139–40, 189
Elizabeth II, queen 131
Ellendun 23
Emlyn, Viscount 79
Emlyn Square 79, 166, 168–9
Empire Theatre 115
Ermin Street 17–18, 20
Euclid Street 144, 195
Even Swindon 24, 26, 104, 125, 164, 188, 191
Ewer, Edward 65
Exeter Street 79

Faringdon 163
Faringdon Road 79, 82, 88, 114–15, 165–6
Farnsby Street 104
Fleet, The 102
Fleet Street 103, 169–70, 174
Fleetway 102, 163, 166
Fleming, Harold 128, 178
Fleming Way 59, 128, 135, 173, 175, 177–8
Folkestone Road 101, 183
Freshbrook 11, 140

Gablecross 137–8
Garrard Engineering 122
Gibbs, C.H. 85
Gilbert's Hill 112, 182

Gloucester 19, 85
Gloucestershire 33, 143
Gluepot pub 169
Goddard, Ambrose 63, 67, 156
Goddard, Pleydell 49
Goddard, Thomas 40, 43, 50
Goddard, family 28, 37, 42, 46, 49, 152–3
Goddard Arms Hotel 44, 93, 154
Golden Lion Bridge 58–9, 102–3, 171, 177
Golden Lion Inn 85, 103, 171
Gooch, Sir Daniel 64–8, 74, 76, 78, 84, 86, 88, 96–7, 104, 113
Gorse Hill 101, 104, 125, 188, 190
Greenbridge 123, 137–8
Greene Fern Farm 111
Greenmeadow 193
Groundwell 23, 26
Groundwell Farm 14–15
Groundwell Ridge 20–1, 145
Groundwell Road 191

Hall, James 115
Handel Street 101
Harcourt Road 101
Harding, family 156
Harding Street 101, 104
Havelock Square 177
Havelock Street 104, 106, 135, 179–80
Hay Lane 62, 64
Haydon 23–4, 140, 144, 192
Haydon Meadow 145
Haydon Street 176
Haydon Wick 22, 26, 189, 193
Heelis (National Trust) 133–4, 169
Henry Street 101, 104
Higford 21
High Street (Old Town) 34–7, 44–8, 79, 83, 93, 149–51, 153–4, 158
High Swindon 11, 24, 28, 39, 42, 152, 164
Highworth 40, 44, 60–1, 122, 127, 150
Historic England 133, 162, 195
Holy Rood Church 36–7, 110, 151–3
Honda 131
Horse Fair 61

Hreod Burna 21
Hudson, Kenneth 120, 145
Huntingdon 156
Hythe Street 101, 183

Iffley Road 101
Ipswich 185
Isis 20

Jefferies, Richard 56, 64, 66, 89, 91, 109–12, 141, 143, 152, 155, 157, 195
John, David Murray (Tower) 68, 121, 131, 164, 180, 189
John Street 101, 104, 183,
Jones, Edmund 101
Junction Station 62, 65, 70, 72, 98, 161, 163

Kennet and Avon Canal 53
Kennet Valley 53
Kent Road 101, 181, 183
Kiln Park 19
King of Prussia Inn 154
King William Street, 183–4
'Kingsbury' 111
Kingsdown 23
Kingshill 101, 104, 125
King's Arms Hotel 48, 154–5

Lacock 38
Lady Lane 22
Lagos Street 176
Lancashire 78, 111
Lansdown Road 183
Latton 54, 175
Lavington, Market 38
Lawn 127, 152
Lawn, The 37, 52, , 151–3
Lechlade 40, 54
Letchworth 188
Lewes 51
Liddington 24
Liddington Wick 26
Liden 127, 139–40, 189, 194
Linslade Street 101
Lister, R.A. 122

Little London 48, 61, 157
Liverpool 63, 78, 84
Lloyd's Bank, High Street 34, 35
Locarno, The 92, 149
London 17, 40, 49, 52–3, 62–4, 68, 72–3, 78–9, 82, 122, 126, 175, 179, 185, 189–91
London, Little 48, 61, 157
London Street 97
Loppos Hill Grounds 65
Loxton, Samuel 4, 116
Lydiard 23, 29
Lydiard House 144–5, 195
Lydiard Millicent 24, 26
Lydiard Park 144, 193, 195
Lydiard Tregoze 24

McArthurGlen outlet centre 137, 169
McIlroys department store 134
Magic Roundabout 54, 59, 127
Maidstone Road 101, 183
Malmesbury 52, 150, 163
Malmesbury Abbey 21
Manchester Road 59, 101, 107–8
Mannington 23, 26
Mantell, George 50–2
Mantell, Gideon 51–2, 60–3, 69
Market Lavington 38
Market Street 179
Marlborough 17, 38, 44, 52, 85, 161
Marlborough Downs 20, 138
Marlborough Road 161, 188, 193
Maxwell Street 101, 166
Maxwell, James 101
Measom, George 70, 72
MECA 186
Mechanics Institute (Institution) 79, 82–3, 86–8, 109, 111–12, 115–16, 120, 167–8, 195
Medgbury Street 176
Melksham 53
Methodist Church, Bath Road 157, 159
Mildenhall 17
Milton Keynes 68, 79, 189
Milton Road 59, 165
Monkton Farleigh 57
Montagu Street 101

Moonrakers junction 191
Moredon 15, 21–4, 26, 126, 140, 188–9
Moredon Road 192
Morris, William 48, 56–7, 63
Morris Motors 122
Morrison, Sydney Bruce 101
Morrison Street 101
Morse, Levi Lapper 182
Motorola 132
Mouldon 23
Mouldon Hill Country Park 144

National Health Service 178
Nationwide Building Society 132, 188, 193
Nethercott 24, 26, 28–9
New Zealand 60
Newbridge Square 135–6
Newport Street 37–9, 48–51, 149–51, 158, 160–1
North Star College 143
North Street 184
North Swindon 22 –3, 137 –8, 141, 144 –5, 188, 189, 192
North Wilts Brewery 154
North Wilts Canal 54 –5, 57, 98, 128, 136, 175
Northumberland 64
Nythe 23, 29, 67, 127
Nyweport 39

Oakhurst 192
Odo, Bishop 26
Okus 27–8, 33, 125, 189, 194
Old Sarum 66
Orbital Retail Park 138, 140, 191–3
Oriel Street 101, 177
Oxford 52, 75, 87, 97, 101, 122, 163, 177
Oxford Brookes University 143
Oxford Street 79

Paddington 52, 82
Parade, The 59, 128, 173, 175, 178
Passmore, Arthur 33
Peatmoor 124, 132
Penhill 22–3, 29, 126, 140, 189–90

Penhill Drive 191
Pewsey 53, 62
Phillips, Bernard 16, 196
Pinehurst 22, 125, 188, 193
Pipers Way 188, 193
Planks, The 151, 159
Plessey 122
Port Sunlight 168
Portland Beds 13, 159
Potter, Beatrix 134
Poundbury 190
Powell, James 'Raggy' 121
Pressed Steel 123
Priestley J.B. 102, 119
Princes Street 60, 185–6
Princess Margaret Hospital 189
Pritchard, Norman 127
Purbeck Beds 13, 40, 159
Purton 11, 19, 22, 141
Purton Road 21

Quarries 28, 34, 39, 41, 49, 52, 60, 93, 159–60
Quarry Road 159
'quaving–gogs' 59
Queen's Drive 127, 191
Queen's Park 34
Queen's Theatre 115
Queenstown 101

Radnor Street Cemetery 113, 180–2, 195
'Raggy' (James Powell) 121
Ramleaze 127
Ray, River 21, 53, 189
Reading 64, 131
Reading Street 79, 169
Redhouse 192
Regent Circus 7, 100, 103–6, 113, 135, 173, 180–1, 184–6
Regent Street 58, 60, 107–8, 134, 171, 177, 179, 185–6
Regent's Park (London) 185
Renault 132
Rhinoceros Inn 157
Ridgeway Farm 141
Rigby, J.D. and C. 72–4, 79, 82–4

INDEX

Rodbourne 125–6, 188, 192
Rodbourne Cheney 24, 26, 126, 192, 196
Rodbourne Road 97–8, 191
Rodbourne Stream 21
Rollestone Street 180
Rushy Platt 59

St Andrew's Ridge 141
St Barnabas Church 191
St Mark's Church 74–5, 78, 85–6, 166
Salisbury 66
Saltaire 168
Sands, The 61, 158
Sanford Street 112, 178
Sarum, Old 66
Savernake Forest 19
Saxon Court 150
Scott, Sir George Gilbert 94, 156
Semington 53, 163
Sevenhampton 40
Severn, River 175
Shaw 15, 23, 140
Shaw Forest Park 144
Shaw Ridge 140
Sheppard, John Harding 183
Sheppard, John Henry Harding 101, 104, 154, 170
Sheppard Street 98
Sheppard's Field 104, 170
Sherston 38
Short Hedge 49, 61, 158
'Silver Book' 127, 139, 141, 197
Smith, W.H. 123
Snell, Edward 74–5, 84–5
Somerset 57, 67
South Marston 15, 23–4, 53, 122, 131, 137, 139
South Street 184
Southampton 161
Sparcells 23
Spectrum 132
Spencer, F.H. 100, 111
Springfield Road 160
Square House 45
Stanton Fitzwarren 19
Station Road 174

STEAM Museum 76–7, 90, 143, 169, 195
Strange, James 50
Strange, Miss, 52
Strange, Thomas 50
Stratton 11, 17, 26, 123, 189
Stratton St Margaret 17, 24, 126–7
Stroud 54
Sturrock, Archibald 76, 78
Sunderland 84
Sussex 51
Sydney Street 101

Tadpole Farm 141–2
Tadpole Lane 21, 140
Tadpole village 142
Taunton Street 79
Taw Hill 140, 192
Tesco (The Parade) 178
Thames, River 40, 52–3, 175, 184
Thames and Severn Canal 54
Thames Valley 64, 138
Thamesdown Borough 21, 120, 132, 138, 140
Theatre Square 58, 135, 185
Thompson, Henry 43
Tismeads 28
Toothill 11, 23, 29, 140, 193
Trafalgar Square 185
Trowbridge 122, 163
Turl Street 101, 177

Union Row 93, 156–7
Union Tavern 175
Unity Place 132–3
Unwin, Raymond 125
Upham Road 191
Upper Eastcott (Farm) 58, 100, 103, 185

Vickers Armstrong 122
Victoria Embankment, London 68, 179
Victoria Road 91, 108–9, 116, 156–8, 184–5
Victoria Street 91, 93, 157
Vilett, family and estate 43, 45, 47, 86, 104–7, 156

Wadard 26
Walcot 16, 26, 28–9, 42, 152–3, 189, 191
Walcot East 126
Walcot West 126
Wales 16, 82, 104, 165
Walmart 138
Wanborough 19, 22, 26, 29, 67, 141
Wantage 62
Wellington Street 176
Welwyn 188
Wessex 21
West Swindon 11, 18, 26–8, 124, 132, 137, 139–40, 144–5, 188–9, 193, 198
Westbury 51
Westcott 24, 26, 28–9, 59
Westcott Place 102, 104
Westlea 139–40
Westleaze 27
Westleaze Farm 27
Westlecot 27, 28, 160–1
Whale Bridge 59, 101–3, 177
Whalebridge junction 176–7
Wharf Bridge 60
Wharf Green 135
Wheeler, Betty 52
White, Ken 102, 177

Whitehead, George 101
Whitehead Street 101
Whitworth Road 22
Wichel, Wichelstowe 11, 27, 141–2, 145, 188–90, 193
Wick Farm 26
Williams, Alfred 102, 120–1, 143, 177
Wilts and Berks Canal 53–4, 56, 63, 67, 104, 141–2, 144, 163, 173, 175, 193
Wilts and Dorset Bank 93, 155
Windmill Hill Business Park 124
Windmill Street 47, 155
Wolverton 68, 79, 168
Wood Street 37–8, 47–8, 61, 93, 154–5, 157–8
Wootton Bassett, Royal 11, 44, 47, 53, 60, 62, 64, 127, 163
Workers' Educational Association 121
Wroughton 10–11, 13, 22, 24, 27, 60, 112, 189, 195
Wyatt, Matthew Digby 82
Wyvern Theatre 143, 146, 186

York Place 100, 185
York Square 108
Yorks Upper Breach 65

Zurich Insurance 132–3, 173

Hobnob Press

Hobnob Press has published more than twenty books about Swindon, and our list of titles about Wiltshire and the surrounding region runs into hundreds. Our Swindon books may be purchased from Swindon Central Library and from local booksellers. Or you can browse our catalogue and order directly from our website: **www.hobnobpress.co.uk**. If you have enjoyed this book you are sure to like its companion volume, **West Swindon: what the eye doesn't see**, by Angela Atkinson, Frances Bevan and Roger Ogle, as well as works by two of its authors, **The Ladies of Lydiard**, by Frances Bevan, and **Swindon, a Born Again Swindonian's Guide**, by Angela Atkinson. Also very relevant are **The Archaeology of the Borough of Swindon**, by Bernard Phillips, and two invaluable reference books by Mark Child, **The Swindon Book**, and **The Swindon Book Companion**. These and all our titles are described in detail on our website.

www.hobnobpress.co.uk